Praise for *Doing It Right*

"Mothers and daughters can agree on *Doing It Right*—nonjudgmental, informative, and easy to understand, it's like a whole semester of sex education in under one hundred and fifty pages."

—Dr. Carol Livoti and Elizabeth Topp,
mother-and-daughter team behind *Vaginas: An Owner's Manual*

"Bronwen Pardes has the courage to tell young teens everything they need to know about their sexuality and responsible sexual expression. A required (and stimulating!) read for all teens—and their parents, too."

—Eric Marcus, author of *Is It a Choice?* and
What if Someone I Know Is Gay?

"Refreshing, honest . . . powerful! This book will make a life-or-death difference to many of today's teens. Browen Pardes writes to inform, not to judge, and she succeeds."

—Bishop John S. Spong, author of
The Sins of Scripture: Exposing the Bible's Texts of Hate to Reveal the God of Love

"This is an informative, highly intelligent look at a teen's changing body, sexuality, and actual physical intimacy. . . . A wonderful guide."

—Teensreadtoo.com

DOING IT RIGHT

BRONWEN PARDES

Simon Pulse
New York London Toronto Sydney

SIMON PULSE

An imprint of Simon & Schuster Children's Publishing Division

1230 Avenue of the Americas, New York, NY 10020

Copyright © 2007 by Bronwen Pardes

SIMON PULSE logo and colophon are registered trademarks of Simon & Schuster, Inc.

Designed by Steve Kennedy and Greg Stadnyk

The text of this book was set in Syntax Serif.

Manufactured in the United States of America

First Simon Pulse edition March 2007

10 9 8 7 6 5 4 3 2 1

Library of Congress Control Number 2006928450

ISBN-13: 978-1-4169-1823-3

ISBN-10: 1-4169-1823-X

For Eric Marcus, my mentor and friend. This is all your fault.

Acknowledgments

· ·

MANY THANKS TO EVERYONE WHO OFFERED ME SUGGESTIONS OR feedback throughout the writing of this book: Mich Bombich, Mary Beth Donnelly, Yael Lipton, Kimberly Lynch, Ryan Marcus, Miriam Richter Matz, Scott Mendelsohn, Shannon Sugarman, future sexologist Biz Kornblum, and my human sexuality students at LaGuardia Community College. And a very special thank-you to Abigail Wolff, Emily Brouwer, and all my 'Tones for their unending confidence.

Thank you to Susan Rowley, Steven Paxton, Juan Olmedo, Arthur Kosmopoulos, and Joanne Rodriguez for teaching me to listen—and therefore write—empathically.

I'd like to thank my parents for not letting me literally be a starving writer; and my brother, Jordan, for the drawing. Thanks to Georgette Weir, the first person who ever hired me to write, and to Brett Wean and Lex Burling for their patient publishing advice. And thank you to David Seldin, not just for the laptop and the desk, but for having faith in this book when it was only an idea.

Special thanks to Melissa Eaton for reading my first draft with a keen sex educator's eye and offering invaluable suggestions. And my eternal gratitude to my dear friend Tara Gorvine, for tying the pencil to my hand and nailing the paper down.

And finally, I am indebted to my agent, Miriam Altshuler, for taking a chance on me, and my editor, Bethany Buck, for making me write a better book than I thought I could. Thank you both for sharing, and never compromising, my vision for this book.

TABLE OF CONTENTS

So . . . Who Are You, Anyway?

I'M A SEXUAL HEALTH EDUCATOR. THAT MEANS I GIVE PEOPLE THE information and skills they need to make healthy, confident decisions about sexuality. I've taught teens about all the subjects in this book.

I teach at junior highs, high schools, and colleges—sometimes in classrooms, and sometimes in more informal workshops where students show up because they heard "The Sex Lady" was coming to campus. My students sometimes get embarrassed about the things I'm teaching, but that's less common than you might think. Mostly they are interested—sex is an interesting subject! And lots of times they want to talk to me privately after class, sometimes to ask me a personal question—"How do I know if my girlfriend is pregnant?" "Do you think I have an STD?"—or to tell me something they haven't told anyone else—"I'm gay, but I'm not out to anyone."

My students have a lot of fun in my classes. There's usually a lot of laughter, which I always encourage, so even when we're talking about difficult or serious subjects, my classroom is usually a happy place. Part of the reason for that is the fact that I love what I do.

People often want to know how I got into this line of work because it's a pretty unusual field. (I have a master's degree in human sexuality, and when I was in graduate school there were only six people in my graduating class.) There are a lot of reasons why I chose to become a sexual health educator:

First of all, when I was in my twenties I had a good friend, named Jim, who died of AIDS. This made me want to help other people prevent HIV and other STDs, and one of the ways to do that is to educate people about how to have safe sex. So in some ways, I do this work in memory of Jim.

Second, when I was in college, I realized that I had a talent for talking to people about sex. My friends would often come to me for advice, not because I was the most experienced (I wasn't) but because I was the most well-informed. I made a point of learning everything I could about sexual health, and I started to realize that I was great at communicating this information to my friends in a way that was both helpful and fun. My college friends like to recall demonstrations I would do for them using a carrot to represent a penis. (The guys always got a little upset if I used a baby carrot.)

I have a strange gift for never being embarrassed—at least not when I'm talking about sex. Recently I had breakfast with one of my best friends and her parents. After the meal was over, when we were alone, my friend said she had been mortified when I mentioned anal sex. It hadn't even occurred to me that that was an unusual topic to discuss over eggs.

So I wanted to do work that helped people and knew I had the odd skill of being able to talk to people about sex without feeling shy. Most important, I knew that the world needs good sexual health educators.

Why do I think it's so important to teach teens about sexuality? Sex is such a vital part of who we are, and teens are at an age when they're just starting to figure it all out. Some of the choices you make now could stay with you for the rest of your life, which is why it's important that they be well-informed and well thought out. Sex can be a wonderful, positive aspect of your life, and it can also lead to some serious consequences. Whether you are sexually active right now or not, whether you're comfortable with your sexuality or still trying to sort it all out, there's lots to know and think about. But there's so much confusing information out there, it's hard to figure out what's true. To add to the confusion, there are lots of people who don't *want* you to have all the information. They're scared that giving teens honest education about sex will make them more likely to do it (this doesn't seem to be true, but lots of people think it is). Other people say they'd be happy to talk to you about sexuality, but they turn out to be too embarrassed. But I'm not embarrassed, and I think that giving you all the facts can only make you safer and healthier.

WHY DID YOU DECIDE TO WRITE THIS BOOK?

Whenever I teach, I learn a lot too, mostly from the kinds of things my students ask me. I've gotten so many questions over the years that I have a good sense of what teens want to know about sexuality. I've compiled all the information I've been asked about into this book so I could reach more people than I do as a teacher. The questions in each chapter are from real teens.

I would have loved a down-to-earth, honest book about sexuality when I was younger, but there were few around. When I grew up and started teaching teens about sex, I still found myself wishing such a book existed so I could suggest it to teens who had questions. I was disappointed in many of the books that did exist. I finally decided that if the book I wished for wasn't out there, I would write it myself.

So why should you listen to me, anyway? I'm not your mother, not a doctor, and you don't even know me. But I hope you'll take what you read in this book to heart for one reason: This book does not tell you what to do. It gives you the information you need, without judgment, to make *your own* decisions about sexuality. There's lots of information you need to know, as you start exploring your sexuality, about how to have sex in a way that's physically and emotionally healthy for you. And there are lots of things you need to figure out for yourself: What's important to you in a sexual partner? What are you ready to do, what are you *not* ready to do, and how do you communicate this to others? This book will help you think about all those things and figure out how *you* feel about them. Because no matter what anyone else tells you, what you do with your body is up to you.

Roanwen Pardes
"The Sex Lady"

DOING IT RIGHT

What Is Sex?

WHAT IS SEX?

PEOPLE ARE ALWAYS TALKING ABOUT IT, BUT WHAT DOES THE WORD really mean? We need to talk about the meanings of a few important words before we can have an honest discussion about sex. In fact, "sex" itself seems like a good one to start with.

The word **sex** has two sets of meanings. For starters, it describes something people do. But there are many different kinds of sex, so how do we know what people mean when they talk about *having* sex? In order to be clear, we need to be more specific. When someone refers to having sex, you might automatically assume they're referring to vaginal sex (a penis entering a vagina). But sex might also mean anal sex (one person's penis penetrating another person's anus) or oral sex (one person's mouth touching another person's penis or vagina). You might also include mutual masturbation—stimulating someone's genitals by hand—in your definition of sex because it's another type of sexual activity that might lead to orgasm.

Then there's the other meaning of the word "sex." Suppose you get an instant message from someone you don't know. You only know their screen name; you can't tell what their real name is. What's one of the first things you want to know about them? You probably want to know what sex they are. In this case, the word "sex" is referring to whether they are male or female. Sometimes people confuse this with a person's **gender**, which is something we'll talk more about in chapter 9.

Sexual Attraction

There are many ways in which we can be attracted to another person—we may think they're nice, or smart, or talented. Feeling attracted to them means we want to get to know them, and we like spending time with them. When we are *sexually* attracted to someone, though, it's a little different—it means we'd like to touch, or kiss, or do other things mentioned in this book with them.

Who we find sexually attractive is in part determined by whether we're attracted to members of the same sex, the opposite sex, or both—in other words, our **sexual orientation**. If a person is **heterosexual**, they are usually attracted to members of the opposite sex. If they are **homosexual**, they are usually attracted to members of the same sex. (They may prefer to be called gay or, in the case of women, lesbians.) People who are attracted to both sexes may consider themselves **bisexual**.

You might find someone sexually attractive because of how they look or smell, or because you like their personality. Or you may find yourself attracted to someone who you *don't* think is good-looking and nice, and you have absolutely no idea why! You might find yourself attracted to certain physical types, or it may just depend on the person. Sexual attraction is a pretty mysterious thing.

Abstinence

Someone who is **abstinent** chooses not to have sex. Some people choose to be abstinent because they don't want to risk pregnancy and STDs, so they avoid having vaginal, anal, or oral sex. Others are abstinent because they feel it's important—either for religious reasons or simply because of their values—to wait until marriage to have intercourse. When people say they're abstinent, keep in mind that the word has different meanings for everyone. People who are abstinent may be okay with other kinds of sexual activity. You can't assume you know what's off-limits for abstinent people unless you ask.

Abstinence is the one surefire way to prevent pregnancy and STDs (assuming your definition of abstinence means no exchange of bodily fluids). Having a safe sexual relationship requires a lot of maturity, and it's admirable to wait until you're older before you take on this responsibility. It's not always easy to be abstinent in a world where lots of people are having sex and there's peer pressure to start getting sexual. But your sex life is your business—if you want to wait until you're older to have sex, don't let anyone talk you out of this decision.

At the same time, if it's *not* your choice to be abstinent and someone is forcing you to promise you won't have sex until you're older or married, it's unlikely you'll stick to this decision for very long. A flimsy commitment to abstinence can sometimes lead to some big mistakes. Let's say you don't read the information in this book about protecting yourself against sexually transmitted diseases because you've decided to be abstinent. If you don't end up sticking to the decision to be abstinent, and you have sex without planning to, you might not know how to do it safely. So whatever you decide, the bottom line is that it's your body and your choice.

Virginity

When I ask people what the word "virgin" means, they usually say "someone who hasn't had sex." But sex might mean vaginal, anal, or oral sex, depending on who you ask. For a lot of people, losing their **virginity** refers to the first time they have vaginal sex—where a penis enters a vagina. That's great for people who want to have that kind of sex. But what about a guy who identifies himself as gay from a young age and never has sex with women? What about a lesbian who has never had sex with men? How might these people define virginity? If the word "virgin" referred to someone who had never had vaginal sex, would they remain virgins no matter how many same-sex partners they had? That probably wouldn't sound right to them.

The word "virgin" seems like it's supposed to describe how sexually experienced you are, but since people don't agree about what it means, it ends up being a pretty useless word. So it's not important to figure out whether that word applies to you—the only thing that matters is what you've done sexually and how you *feel* about what you've done.

Sexuality

Of all the words I've defined so far, this is probably the toughest one to understand, but here's a way to look at it. . . .

Think for a moment about who you are. Are you shy or outgoing? Funny or serious? High-energy or low-key? How do you express these things to the world? Do you approach people and start conversations, or do you like to be alone? Are you bubbly and energetic, or are you usually chilling on a sofa? Is your clothing style preppy, sloppy, or totally unique? Who do you hang out with? What do you like to do with your friends? All these things make up your personality.

The word "sexuality" is another very broad term that describes all the aspects of who you are as a sexual being, much like the word "personality" describes all the different aspects of who you are as a person. All the stuff I've mentioned in this chapter, and more, is a part of your **sexuality**. Are you a male or a female (your sex)? Are you attracted to the same sex, the opposite sex, or both (your sexual orientation)? Do you have a lot of sexual experience, or a little, or none? Have you enjoyed the sexual experiences you've had so far? What turns you on? What turns you off? When someone else is talking about sex, do you blush, or do you join the conversation? Do you flirt? You may not even be sure of the answers to some of these questions, but this book will help you think about them. And thinking about them will help you make mature, informed decisions about sex.

You may be noticing there's a lot more to these terms than you thought when you first picked up this book. The definitions aren't hard and fast; they are different depending on who you talk to. I'm not here to define them for you, but to help you figure out what they mean to you.

One final word about this book: Some of the things you read about here will sound exciting, some will sound strange, some will sound funny, and some will sound downright gross. Maybe you've done some of the things mentioned in this book, maybe there are some you haven't done but want to, and maybe there are some you don't think you'll ever want to do. All the things I address in this book are here because real teens have asked me about them. The most important thing for you to take from reading about them is that it's okay to want to do these things, or *not* to want to. As long as you're being safe and both parties can and do consent, what you choose to do, or not to do, is up to you.

2 The Lowdown on Down Below: Reproductive Anatomy

BEFORE WE TALK ABOUT SEX, WE NEED TO TALK ABOUT THE PARTS OF the male and female reproductive anatomy—what they look like and what they do. I'll also explain two major reproductive functions that you're probably already experiencing—**menstruation** for girls and making *spermatozoa* (what most people call sperm) for boys. Before you can understand how these things happen, you'll need to know about all the parts of the anatomy involved in those processes. You may already have learned all this in a biology class. You may even have found it boring, if science isn't your favorite subject. However, if you're thinking about becoming sexually active, this isn't stuff you need to memorize for an exam, it's stuff you need to learn so you understand how your body (and your partner's body) works.

BOYS

When boys go through puberty, their testicles start making sperm, and they continue to do so, whether they use it or not, for the rest of their lives. Most of the parts you see in the diagram on the next page have to do with how the body makes sperm and how it releases sperm out of the **penis** during sexual activity.

So here's what's happening in a boy's body on a continual basis: Sperm are created in the **testicles** (which are contained in a soft pouch called the **scrotum**). They then move to the **epididymis**, a tubelike structure behind each testicle, where they develop and grow. From there they go to the **vas deferens**, where they wait to travel up and out of the body during ejaculation. When a guy is going to ejaculate, the sperm travel up the vas deferens to the **ejaculatory duct**, which is where the sperm wait to get released from the body by muscle contractions. When the guy ejaculates, the **prostate** and **seminal vesicle** also release fluids, which mix with the sperm. What comes out is a milky white fluid (semen) that contains somewhere between one hundred and seven hundred million sperm.

It's easy to confuse the terms **semen** and **sperm**, so let's clear that up: Sperm are tiny cells made in the testicles. If they meet with an egg inside the female body, the girl may become pregnant. When a guy **ejaculates** (when he has an orgasm and releases fluid from his penis, or "cums"—more on this in chapter 13), what comes out of the penis is called semen—the fluid that contains, among other things, millions of sperm.

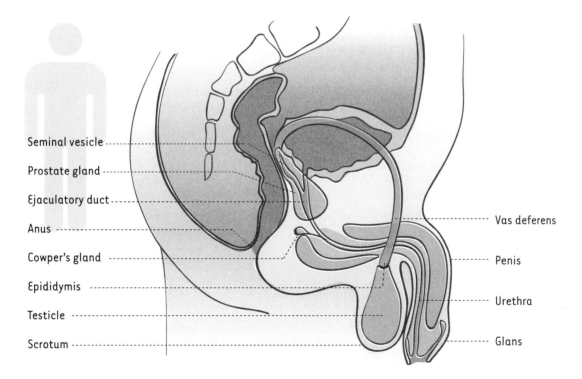

Seminal vesicle

Prostate gland

Ejaculatory duct

Anus

Cowper's gland

Epididymis

Testicle

Scrotum

Vas deferens

Penis

Urethra

Glans

Before ejaculation, the **Cowper's gland** may release a little bit of clear fluid called **pre-ejaculate** (not all guys have this, but many do). The purpose of this fluid is to clean out the inside of the **urethra**, since it's also a place where urine, or pee, travels. Beware—pre-ejaculate can contain enough sperm to get someone pregnant!

TERMS

Anus: where feces, or poop, comes out of

Cowper's gland: a little organ that secretes pre-ejaculate, or pre-cum, a fluid that helps clean out the urethra before ejaculation

Ejaculatory duct: the place where sperm wait to get expelled from the body during ejaculation

Epididymis: tubes around the testicles where sperm are stored until they're ready to leave the body

Glans: the end of the penis, which may be an especially sensitive spot

Penis: the male sex organ. When a guy gets turned on, it fills up with blood and gets bigger and harder.

Prostate: a gland that makes some of the fluid in semen

Scrotum: the sack that contains the testicles

Seminal vesicle: an organ that makes some of the fluid in semen

Testicles: two round organs, about the size of walnuts, in which sperm are made

Urethra: the tube inside the penis; semen and urine come out of it

Vas deferens: the tube that carries sperm from the epididymis

GIRLS

The diagram below shows the **vulva**—that's the word for the outer area of the female genitals. For a girl, looking at the vulva is probably easiest with a mirror. The **outer lips**, or **labia majora**, are easily visible, and gently spreading them apart reveals the **inner lips**, or **labia minora**, and the **clitoris**. The clitoris is a small but very sensitive organ that feels extremely pleasurable when stimulated. Under the clitoris is the **urethra**, where urine comes out of, and, a bit below it, the opening to the **vagina**, where a penis, dildo, or a finger or two might go during sexual activity. Because so much of the important female anatomy is on the inside, the diagrams on pages ten and eleven show the internal anatomy.

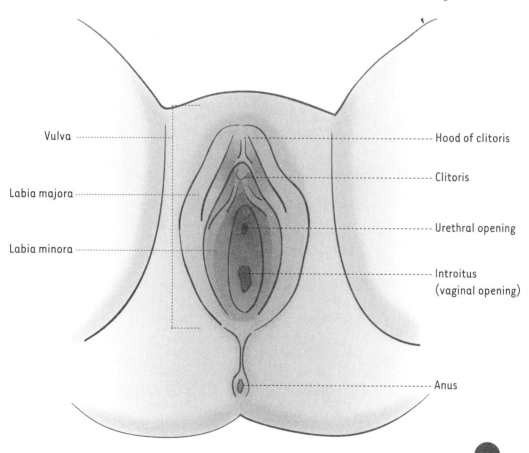

Vulva

Labia majora

Labia minora

Hood of clitoris

Clitoris

Urethral opening

Introitus
(vaginal opening)

Anus

reproductive **anatomy**

Each month a girl goes through a process that gives her body a chance to make a baby. This process is called the **menstrual cycle**, and here's how it works:

A girl's **ovaries** contain thousands of tiny eggs—she is born with all the eggs she'll ever have. Every month a tiny egg pops out of one of her ovaries and travels down the **fallopian tube**. This is called **ovulation**. If that egg meets up with a sperm while in the fallopian tube, the girl might get pregnant (but that's a story for chapter 6). For now we'll assume the egg travels through the fallopian tube without meeting a sperm and heads down to the **uterus**, which is the place where a baby would grow.

Meanwhile, other important stuff has been going on in her uterus.

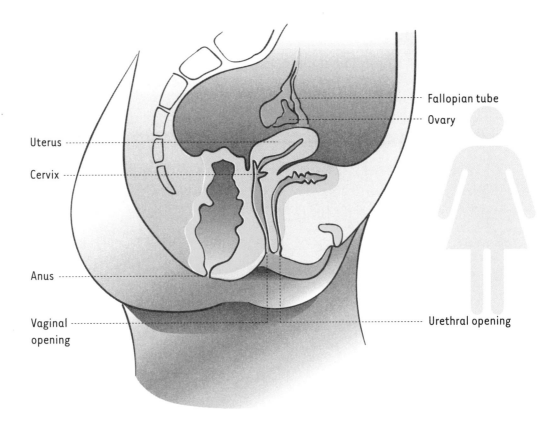

Each month a thick layer of tissue builds up on the inner walls of her uterus, getting it ready to be home to a baby if she does get pregnant. But most months the egg gets down to the uterus without meeting a sperm. Since the girl doesn't need the lining anymore, the uterus contracts, or squeezes, and blood comes out her vagina. That's why girls bleed for a few days each month (and the squeezing is why they may get cramps). Then the process starts all over again.

Each cycle lasts somewhere around twenty-eight days. Keep in mind that everyone's body is different—particularly during adolesence, a girl's cycle may be longer or shorter than that, and it may be different every month. But here's how the timing works for a girl who has a twenty-eight-day cycle: The day she gets her period (starts to bleed) is the first day of the

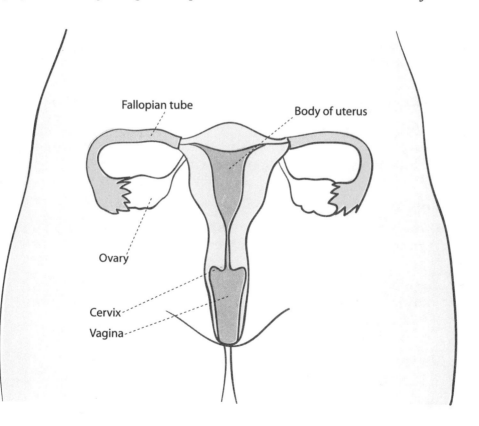

cycle. She will usually bleed for roughly five days. She will ovulate (release an egg) somewhere in the middle of the cycle—roughly the fourteenth day. If she doesn't get pregnant, two more weeks will go by, and the cycle will start over—she will start to bleed again.

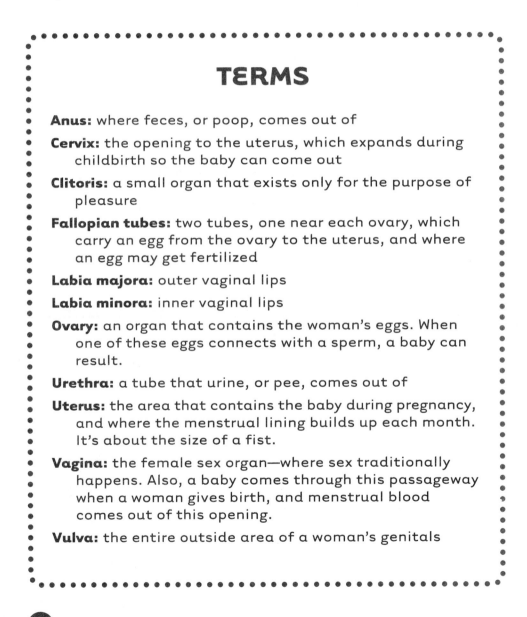

TERMS

Anus: where feces, or poop, comes out of

Cervix: the opening to the uterus, which expands during childbirth so the baby can come out

Clitoris: a small organ that exists only for the purpose of pleasure

Fallopian tubes: two tubes, one near each ovary, which carry an egg from the ovary to the uterus, and where an egg may get fertilized

Labia majora: outer vaginal lips

Labia minora: inner vaginal lips

Ovary: an organ that contains the woman's eggs. When one of these eggs connects with a sperm, a baby can result.

Urethra: a tube that urine, or pee, comes out of

Uterus: the area that contains the baby during pregnancy, and where the menstrual lining builds up each month. It's about the size of a fist.

Vagina: the female sex organ—where sex traditionally happens. Also, a baby comes through this passageway when a woman gives birth, and menstrual blood comes out of this opening.

Vulva: the entire outside area of a woman's genitals

Puberty

· ·

IF YOU'RE READING THIS BOOK, THEN YOU'VE PROBABLY ALREADY started going through puberty. You may be noticing changes that are happening to your body, and you may like them, or hate them, or both. You may be a girl who hates being taller than the guys in her class, or a guy who hates being shorter than the girls. You may feel like your body has been changing way too quickly, or not quickly enough, or not as quickly as your friends' bodies.

During this time, girls are getting their periods and boys' bodies are starting to make sperm—this means your bodies are becoming ready to reproduce. Babies might be the furthest thing from your mind right now, but another way your body starts to prepare for making babies is that you are starting to think more about sex. The hormones that are creating all these physical changes in your body are also having an effect on your thoughts and feelings.

GIRLS

Because girls tend to start puberty earlier than boys (girls start between the ages of nine and thirteen, while boys start between ten and sixteen), and because it tends to start with a growth spurt, a girl may be taller than some boys her age for a short time. Eventually most boys catch up—and since they grow for longer, they end up being taller than most girls.

Girls have started developing breasts and wearing bras. Their bodies are getting curvier—their hips, thighs, and butts may get bigger, and they're starting to look less like kids and more like women. It's important to remember that these changes in body shape are normal; if she can't fit into the same pair of pants she wore a few months ago, that doesn't necessarily mean she's gaining weight inappropriately. In fact, she might not be gaining weight at all—just changing shape.

She's started getting hair in new places—especially under her arms and around her vulva. Many girls shave the hair under their arms and on their legs—there is no medical need to shave this hair; it's simply her choice, and is a custom in most Western countries.

That Time of the Month

Somewhere around two or three years after puberty begins, a girl will start to get her period (for more information, go back to chapter 2). This happens any time between the ages of eight and sixteen. If she approaches the age of sixteen and hasn't gotten her period, she should speak to a gynecologist who can help find out if anything is wrong.

The standard menstrual cycle is twenty-eight days long—that's the number of days between the first day of one period and the first day of the next period. But everyone is different. In fact, a girl's cycle may be different from month to month. Lots of things can throw off the rhythm of a menstrual cycle—stress, or a change in diet, exercise routine, or sleep habits.

If a girl is not sexually active, there's no need for concern about pregnancy if her period is irregular. If she *is* sexually active, it's important to understand how this cycle works and to use birth control during intercourse. She should pay attention if she misses a period—that could be the first sign of pregnancy. (You can read more about preventing pregnancy in chapter 6.)

It's common for teenage girls to have irregular cycles under any circumstances. As girls get older, their cycles usually become more regular. If a girl starts skipping one or more periods on a regular basis, or if the irregularity seems like a cause for concern, she should talk to a doctor.

Many girls experience premenstrual syndrome (PMS)—a set of symptoms such as depression, irritability, cramps, breast tenderness, and discomfort that occur for a few days before getting their periods. The menstrual cycle is controlled by hormones, chemical messengers in the body that control reproductive functions, and these hormones have a big effect on our moods. Right before a girl gets her period each month, the levels of some important hormones change dramatically. As a result, she may become depressed or stressed out.

Some girls don't get these feelings at all. Others get what you might call a "mild case" of PMS. And some have a severe case of PMS, to the point where they may feel or seem like a different person for a few days.

What can help with PMS? The birth control pill can sometimes be helpful, even for someone who isn't sexually active, because it regulates hormones so the changes in hormone levels aren't as extreme. In some severe cases, antidepressant medication is prescribed. If PMS is making it difficult for a girl to function, she should see a doctor. If it's noticeable but not too bad, she could try to exercise regularly (which is always good for mental health anyway), and give in to the chocolate cravings if it helps.

Once a girl gets her period each month, she can say good-bye to PMS and hello to menstrual cramps. Why does this happen? A girl gets her period because the lining that builds up in her uterus over the course of a month—which would help nurture a baby if she got pregnant—is shedding. To release this lining, the uterus has to contract, or squeeze. These contractions can sometimes cause a dull ache in her abdomen. Cramps can also be caused by the hormones that are present in large amounts in her body during this time.

Most girls only get cramps for a few days. Over-the-counter pain relievers, regular exercise, and a hot bath are all good solutions. If the cramps are severe, she should see a doctor.

Tampons or Pads?

Many girls prefer tampons because they feel neater and less bulky. However, tampons can be difficult to put in the first time, so pads can be great for younger girls who are still getting used to having a period.

If a girl is using a tampon for the first time, I suggest she get to know her genitals first. She can check herself out in a mirror using the diagram in chapter 2 as a guide. This is easiest if she's relaxed—laying down and taking deep breaths can help. If she's relaxed and knows where her vagina is, the tampon should slide right in. (The string should stay on the outside so it will be easier to take out later.)

One danger associated with tampons is toxic shock syndrome, a rare but serious illness that can be caused by tampon use. For safety purposes, a girl should change her tampon every four to eight hours even if it's not saturated, and should use a pad when she's asleep to avoid leaving a tampon in for too long. She shouldn't use tampons that are more absorbent than she needs. In other words, if the tampon isn't saturated after a few hours, she probably needs a less absorbent one. She will probably want to have a variety of grades of tampons on hand every month, because periods tend to start out heavy and get lighter after a couple of days. Finally, if she gets a fever while using a tampon, she should remove it immediately and see a doctor.

When using a tampon, a girl can swim without worry during her period and she can stay in the water as long as she wants (as long as she remembers to change the tampon every four to eight hours)—it will not get soaked with water. (If it *does* seem to be soaked when she takes it out, that's from being inside of her vagina, not from swimming.) And if the tampon has been inserted properly and has been changed, it should not fall out during swimming.

There are many alternatives to the menstrual products found in your local drug store, such as The Keeper and the The DivaCup, which are cups that are inserted into the vagina to hold menstrual blood. These products have the advantage of being more environmentally friendly than the ones most people are used to—either they're reusable, or they're chemical-free and are made of biodegradable materials.

There are some who say that the chemicals used to bleach tampons are harmful to the vagina, and that the convenience of using tampons is not worth the risk of toxic shock syndrome. Alternative menstrual products can help a girl avoid the risks associated with using tampons. Also, menstrual cups last a long time and cut down on the cost of tampons or pads.

On the other hand, menstrual cups can be a little more difficult to use than tampons. And while tampons absorb blood, menstrual cups store it, which can get messier when it comes to removal.

If a girl is allergic to latex, she should make sure to use a menstrual cup made of silicone or another material. Using these products is mostly a matter of adjusting to them, feeling comfortable having more contact with menstrual blood, and being willing to be a bit of a pioneer.

If she doesn't want to use the menstrual cup but wants a more natural tampon, there are tampons that aren't bleached—the only reason to bleach them is for the sake of appearance, and bleach contains some chemicals that some girls would rather not put in their vaginas. These are often available in the hygiene section of health food stores.

When to visit the gyno

A girl should start seeing a gynecologist when she becomes sexually active, when she reaches the age of eighteen regardless of sexual activity, or if at sixteen she hasn't yet gotten her period. It's normal for her to be nervous about her first exam, but it only takes a few minutes.

When she calls to make the appointment, she should let the receptionist know that it's her first appointment, and whether she prefers a male or a female doctor. On her first visit, the doctor will start out by taking her medical history, including information about sexual activity.

In the exam room, the doctor will ask her to lay down and put her feet up in stirrups. If this part makes her nervous, she can try taking long, deep breaths. The doctor will insert a metal instrument called a speculum into her vagina in order to see the cervix. He or she will then take some cells from the cervix to see if there are any cells there that might become cancerous (this is very rare for teenage girls, but it becomes more important with age). For a sexually active patient, the doctor will take another sample to test for STDs.

The next part is called a bimanual exam—the doctor will insert one or two fingers inside the vagina and use the other hand to put some pressure on the belly—this is how she checks the internal reproductive organs (uterus, fallopian tube, and ovaries). The doctor may also check the rectum, by inserting a finger into the anus, and will also check the breasts for lumps.

While some parts of the exam may cause a little discomfort, they should not cause any pain—if they do, the girl should tell her doctor. She should feel comfortable speaking with the doctor honestly about sexual activity, birth control, her period, STDs, and anything else on her mind (if she doesn't volunteer this information, the doctor will not be able to tell for certain from examining her whether she's had sex or masturbated). If a girl is concerned about her doctor sharing information with her parents, she might try finding out if her town has a clinic or a Planned Parenthood that will see her without parental consent.

One final word: Any doctor should answer a patient's questions patiently and in simple terms. He or she should be attentive and responsive. If you don't feel comfortable with your doctor, it's your right to find a new one.

Breasts

Just like guys and their penises, girls can get pretty wrapped up in the size of their breasts, whether they think they've got giant boobs or tiny tits. But the truth is, the size of our breasts is predetermined by genetics, and if someone's unhappy with theirs, there isn't a lot one can do.

There are lots of products that claim to make breasts bigger. Some of them, like breast-enhancement creams, just don't work. Others, like implants, carry a lot of risks—some we know about, and more we'll probably find out about in the future. The truth is, breasts may change size with weight gain or loss, but otherwise, a girl is pretty much stuck with them. Her best bet is to accept them as they are, and on occasion, wear a padded bra for a little extra help if she wants.

Big breasts can be a pain, especially when it comes time to buy bras. The best place to buy them is a lingerie store, where salespeople can determine the appropriate size and help customers find brands that work for their bodies.

Big boobs can be especially annoying for girls who play sports or work out. Athletic girls should try making an investment in a couple of good sports bras—www.titlenine.com is one website that sells sports bras for athletic women of all sizes. Some athletes will even wear two bras at a time for better support.

If that doesn't help, breast-reduction surgery is another option. It may be covered by health insurance if the girl is able to claim that the size of her breasts is causing her physical difficulties, such as back pain. However, this surgery, like any other, comes with some risks. It will involve considerable recovery time, and there's a chance breast sensation will be permanently lost. There's also the possibility she wouldn't be able to breast-feed if she becomes a mother. This is a decision that requires a great deal of consideration. A plastic surgeon can offer more in-depth information.

If your breasts are different sizes, rest assured that almost no one is perfectly symmetrical. A good shoe salesperson will tell you that very few people have feet that are exactly the same size (though I rarely get asked about lopsided feet). In fact, roughly 40 percent of all women have breasts that are slightly different sizes. Short of an invasive procedure, which I don't recommend, there isn't anything girls can do about lopsided breasts except name them accordingly.

Some girls are especially embarrassed about hair on their breasts. One of the trials of puberty is that hair appears in lots of different places, and sometimes in places that feel especially wrong, like breasts. A girl can just let it be, cut it, or pluck it. She should just be very careful, especially if the hair is on her nipples, which are particularly sensitive.

QUESTIONS

My labia kind of hang down. Is this normal?

Yup! There's as much difference in how vulvae look as there is in how faces look, and just because yours looks a little different from those you've seen in this book or elsewhere doesn't mean there's anything wrong with yours. If you don't believe me, check out a copy of Betty Dodson's *Sex for One*, a book about masturbation in which she includes sketches of vulvae of all different shapes and sizes.

I get sort of a creamy, yellowish discharge in my underwear. Is something wrong?

Discharge from the vagina is all part of your body's natural cleansing process. If you don't have your period yet, an increase in discharge may be a sign that you're going to get it soon. The discharge may be clear, milky, or yellowish. It may be sticky or watery, depending on the time of the month. If it starts to increase dramatically or smell different, you should consult a doctor, but otherwise it's completely natural.

What is douche, and should I use it?

No. Douche is a liquid that's inserted into the vagina with a pump in order to clean it. Some women think this will keep their vagina clean and make it smell nicer. The truth is, your vagina has a natural cleansing process that's better than any product you can buy. Douches alter the natural, healthy balance of the bacteria in your vagina. Some people also believe they can be helpful in preventing pregnancy or STDs, but this is absolutely not true.

The best thing you can do is wash your vulva gently with mild soap and warm water, and let your body take care of the rest. Keep in mind that your vulva may have an odor, but that's natural. If you notice any changes in the smell or are concerned about it, see a doctor rather than trying to take care of it yourself.

BOYS

Puberty usually starts between ages ten and sixteen with a growth spurt—not only does a boy get taller, but his shoulders get broader, and his muscles may get bigger. His testicles and penis grow as well.

Boys are seeing hair in new places—around the penis, under the arms, and on the face. They may be anxious to start shaving, as this is one of the most obvious signs of manhood. Their voices starts growing deeper, which may involve some cracks and squeaks along the way.

Doctor Visits

It's a good idea for a guy to see his internist when he starts having sex. The doctor will examine his genitals, feeling the testicles, scrotum, and penis for lumps. If a guy feels any pain during this exam, he should let the doctor know. The doctor should also teach a guy how to examine himself for testicular cancer—this type of cancer is most common between ages eighteen and thirty-four, and can be easily detected and treated if caught early, which a guy can do by checking his testicles every month. The doctor may also do a rectal exam, which will involve inserting a lubricated finger into the anus. This may be a little uncomfortable, but it will be quick, and taking some long, deep breaths can help.

A guy should feel free to talk to his doctor about birth control, STDs, or whatever else is on his mind.

The Penis

Circumcision

When a boy is born, some parents make the decision to circumcise him—that is, to remove the foreskin, which is a flap of skin that covers the penis. Roughly 60 percent of boys in this country are circumcised. Some religions (Judaism and Islam, for example) circumcise as a matter of custom. Others do it because they believe the penis will be healthier or cleaner if circumcised, though the truth is, there is not a significant difference either way. Lots of dads make the decision based on whether or not *they* were circumcised, so their son's penis looks like theirs.

If a guy isn't circumcised, he may notice that a whitish, cheesy substance can form under the foreskin. This is called *smegma*, and it cleans and lubricates the penis. He may notice that more smegma is being produced once he starts puberty. He can wash it away by retracting the foreskin to clean the head of the penis.

Erections

An erection is what happens when a guy is aroused—his penis gets hard. (For more information on how that happens, take a look at chapter 13.) A teenage guy may get erections even when he's not aroused, and it sometimes seems like that happens at the worst possible times (like when he's standing in front of the entire class and wearing sweatpants). If he tries to ignore it, it should go away pretty quickly—he can try thinking about something else, maybe something that is very unsexy. Although an unwanted erection can be a pain, this will stop happening when his hormones settle down. In the meantime, he should keep in mind that it's a sign everything is working well down there.

Most healthy guys wake up in the morning with an erection too. Some even have several erections each night during the deep sleep phase called rapid eye movement (REM) when he's dreaming. Girls also have periods of arousal during the night, but they're not as pronounced as in guys because erections are very noticeable. Guys may also ejaculate in their sleep (see the question later in this chapter on wet dreams).

Does Size Matter?

The average penis ranges in size from about five to seven inches. Some are a little bigger than that and some are a little smaller.

A guy's penis and testicles usually get bigger during puberty. Once they stop growing, there isn't anything he can do to make them grow. Penis size, like height, is based on genetics.

It's difficult to tell from the size of a soft penis how big it is when it's erect and hard. That's a good thing to tell someone who makes a mean comment in a locker room. As far as having sex is concerned, there's no reason for people to place so much emphasis on penis size. Anyone, big or small, can satisfy a partner by finding out what makes him or her feel good.

And bigger isn't always better—some guys worry their penis is too big. There isn't anything anyone can do about that, either. If the size of a guy's penis is making sex difficult, I suggest he use a lot of lubricant and go slowly at first to give his partner a chance to adjust to the size of his penis.

QUESTIONS

My penis curves when it's erect. Is that normal?

Yes, lots of penises look a little curved when they're erect. Unless it causes you pain during intercourse, there's nothing to worry about.

I think I had a wet dream. What exactly is it, and why does it happen?

A wet dream is simply a sexy dream that makes a guy get an erection and ejaculate in his sleep. When he wakes up, if he's not sure what happened, he may think he wet the bed. Girls can have sexy dreams that get them aroused too, but because there's less fluid involved, there's less evidence that she was aroused.

Wet dreams are absolutely normal. They'll probably happen most often while you're going through puberty and less often as you get older, especially if you're having sex and masturbating (and therefore doing enough ejaculating during the day). There's no need to worry, but if you feel embarrassed about them, this is probably a great time for you to learn to wash your own sheets.

I'm a guy, and I think I'm developing breasts. It's embarrassing! Is this normal?

Yes, it's normal, and it's almost always a temporary thing.

As you go through puberty, the changes that happen in your body are due to hormones. Hormones called androgens are responsible for most of the changes that happen to guys, and estrogens are responsible for most of the girl characteristics, including breasts. But girls have a small amount of androgens, and guys have a small amount of estrogens. Some guys, as they're going through puberty, have enough estrogens to cause them to develop breasts, which may feel a little bit tender. This happens to some degree to roughly half of all guys, and in almost all cases it goes away in a few months to two years (if it seems to last a long time, see a doctor). It can be embarrassing, but loose shirts will help to cover it up.

4 Am I Ready?

Am I Ready?

IN CHAPTER 3 WE TALKED ABOUT PUBERTY AND WHAT HAPPENS TO YOUR body as you grow from a child into an adult. All those changes—breasts growing, hair appearing in new places, changes in your genitals, getting your period, having your first wet dream—mean that your body is ready to have sex. Being physically ready is one thing, but how do you know if you're ready *emotionally*? The fact that you're reading this chapter probably means you're asking yourself this question.

Becoming sexually active is a big deal. Having sex can be a great experience. But it also comes with a lot of consequences. Sexually transmitted diseases and unwanted pregnancy are very real risks, so you'll want to make sure you're informed and ready to take precautions (you can learn how in chapters 5 and 6).

In addition, sex can bring on a lot of feelings you might not be prepared for. If you have sex with someone you feel really strongly about, those feelings might deepen if you have sex with them—which can be both wonderful and a little scary. If you have sex with someone you don't feel that strongly about, you could find yourself feeling more attached to them, whether you want to or not.

I'm not trying to discourage you from having sex. But I want to be sure that if you do, you'll think about it carefully.

For starters, why do you want to have sex? There may be lots of reasons:

◎ You have a steady girlfriend or boyfriend, you've been getting closer to each other, and sex just feels like the natural next step.

◎ You're curious—everyone is talking about sex, and now you want to experience it for yourself.

◎ You're just plain horny! Sex is all you can think about, and you'd rather do it than think about it.

◎ You feel you're old enough. Sex is something people your age do.

But maybe you're not sure if you're ready. Everyone is different, and everyone feels ready at different times. The important thing is not to have sex before you are ready, and only you can figure out when that is.

DOES AGE MATTER?

The law tells you when you're old enough to drink, drive, and vote, and believe it or not, it has rules about when you're old enough to consent to sex, too. Someone above the age of consent who has sex with someone below the age of consent can be charged with a crime. Age of consent varies from state to state, but in most states it ranges from sixteen to eighteen. For specific information on your state, go to www.avert.org/aofconsent.htm, and for more information on consent, see chapter 14.

Lots of people consent to sex before they're allowed to according to the law. Young people don't usually get into legal trouble for having sex with another young person unless someone (like a parent) presses charges, but it's something to keep in mind when making the decision to have sex.

That being said, no one can tell you an age when you're ready to have sex. There can be lots of pressure, but the only good reason to do it is because you know you're ready. If you don't know that, then wait. Having sex can make you feel very grown-up. But here's another thing that can make you feel grown-up: making your own decision, one that's right for you, no matter what other people around you are doing.

READY OR NOT, HERE I COME!

You may not be ready, but maybe your partner *is*. It can be tough having a boyfriend or girlfriend who is ready for sex when you're not. That's a situation requiring a very honest conversation. Talk about why you don't feel ready, and ask for patience. In addition, talk about the ways you can be close without having intercourse, and be clear about what kinds of touching you *are* comfortable with. You will have to do some serious talking in this conversation, but make sure you do a lot of listening, too. Even talking about the ways you enjoy touching each other can feel very intimate. You can both feel close to each other, and satisfy each other, without having intercourse until you're ready.

Even if you're sure you want to wait, it can get tougher as you get older—if lots of your friends and classmates are doing it and you're not, you can start to feel left out, like they all belong to a secret club and you're not a member. But keep this in mind: By the time they graduate from high school, roughly 60 percent of all teenagers have had sex. This means that 40 percent of your peers *haven't* had sex by that time. You're far from being the only one.

Sex is a very intimate act. It's a great way of expressing strong feelings for someone, and also a great way of developing *even stronger* feelings for them. If you want to have that experience with someone you love and trust, then hopefully that will feel more important than what your friends and classmates are doing. At the end of the day, your sex life matters only to you and the people you have sex with.

If you're thinking about having sex for the first time and are feeling confused, here are some questions to consider:

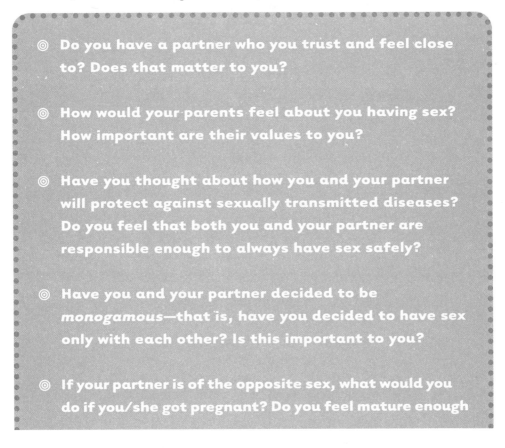

◎ **Do you have a partner who you trust and feel close to? Does that matter to you?**

◎ **How would your parents feel about you having sex? How important are their values to you?**

◎ **Have you thought about how you and your partner will protect against sexually transmitted diseases? Do you feel that both you and your partner are responsible enough to always have sex safely?**

◎ **Have you and your partner decided to be *monogamous*—that is, have you decided to have sex only with each other? Is this important to you?**

◎ **If your partner is of the opposite sex, what would you do if you/she got pregnant? Do you feel mature enough** to handle the big decisions and responsibilities that would come along with that? Is abortion an option? How do you feel about having a child or giving a child up for adoption? You need to consider not just how *you* feel about these decisions but how your partner feels as well.

◎ *Why* do you want to have sex? Sometimes it seems like everyone else is doing it and you start to feel left out. But sex is a very private thing. When you think about it, what you do or don't do sexually is really no one else's business.

◎ Why *now*? Are you in a more serious relationship than you've ever been in before? Are you in love? Do you just feel ready?

◎ Is your partner pressuring you to have sex? No one has the right to pressure you to have sex before you're ready. If you're scared this person will break up with you if you don't say yes, that's a good sign that *you* should break up with *them*. If you feel threatened in any way, tell an adult immediately.

◎ How do you *feel* about having sex? What emotions come up when you think about it? Are you excited or scared? Trust your feelings. If the thought makes you feel more nervous than happy, that might be a sign that you should wait a while longer.

doing it right

Before you make this decision, I suggest you talk to an adult you trust, if possible. There's no way to anticipate all the very strong feelings that sex can bring on. Someone older—a relative, a counselor at your school, an older friend or neighbor—can offer some perspective.

QUESTIONS

I'm underage and I know I'm not supposed to drink, but if I'm nervous about having sex for the first time, would having a couple of drinks help?

Although I won't preach to you about underage drinking, I can tell you that alcohol tends to make sex worse rather than better. It can affect your body's ability to become aroused—this means you may have trouble getting or keeping an erection or reaching orgasm. Alcohol can also cloud your judgment, making it more likely you'll do things you wouldn't have done otherwise, and more likely that you'll forget what you know about safer sex (more on this in chapter 5). In the majority of date rapes, the victim, the assaulter, or both were drinking or on some other kind of drug. Finally, alcohol dulls sensation—you're about to do something that feels really good, and this is no time to dampen your senses! If you're too nervous to have sex sober, think about whether that's a sign that you're not ready, or think about other ways you can get over your nerves.

I can't wait to have sex for the first time! My partner and I don't love each other, but we both want to have sex just for the experience. Should we do it, or should we wait?

It sounds like you feel you're ready for sex, and you have a trustworthy and willing partner. This is a pretty good scenario for having sex for the first time.

But I'm curious about why you're so eager to have sex. Is it because so many others around you are having sex? Or is it because *you* want to?

Of course sex —the first time or any time—doesn't have to be with someone you love. But one reason sex and love often go hand in hand is because having sex with someone— especially your *first* someone—can bring on a lot of very strong feelings, maybe more feelings than you'd expect.

I recommend a little soul-searching: Which is more important, having sex now, or having it with someone you love? Whatever you decide is okay as long as you feel sure it's what you both want.

No Glove, No Love: Protecting Against STDs

WHAT'S SAFER SEX?

SAFER SEX MEANS PROTECTING YOURSELF AND YOUR PARTNER FROM STDS (sexually transmitted diseases, which you can read more about in chapter 11). When I say something is "unsafe," that means it involves some risk of transmitting an STD (either getting one if your partner has one, or passing one along if you have one). The only surefire way to stay STD-free is to be abstinent. If you do choose to have sex, know that sex is never perfectly safe, but you can use the precautions discussed in this chapter to make it safer. It's your responsibility to talk about safer sex practices with your partner and take care of your health and theirs. You can reduce the risk of STD transmission by putting a barrier between yourself and your partner every time you have oral, anal, or vaginal sex. This chapter will give you the information you need to be as safe as possible; the rest is up to you.

Condoms

A condom is a device usually made of latex that covers the penis during sex. It can be used for any type of sex that involves a penis—vaginal sex, anal sex, or oral sex. The major advantage of condoms is that they protect against both pregnancy and STDs. They're very easy to use, but it's a great idea to practice using one before you're in the heat of the moment—it's always a bit harder to put one on when you're turned on or nervous. Try practicing on a cucumber, a banana, or, if you have a penis, on yourself. Girls, if you plan to have sex with boys, this means you, too—there's no rule that says the guy has to be the only one who knows how.

Before you open the packaging of a condom, there are a couple of things you should do:

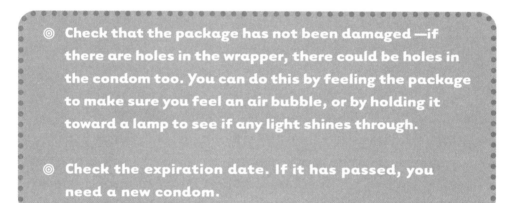

◎ **Check that the package has not been damaged —if there are holes in the wrapper, there could be holes in the condom too. You can do this by feeling the package to make sure you feel an air bubble, or by holding it toward a lamp to see if any light shines through.**

◎ **Check the expiration date. If it has passed, you need a new condom.**

If you're good to go, your next steps should happen once there's an erection:

◎ **Open the packaging carefully using your hands. It may look cool to open it with your teeth, but a torn condom isn't worth that one moment of coolness.**

◎ **Remove the condom from the package and check to see which side is up. If you accidentally put it on wrong side up (you'll know if you can't roll it down),**

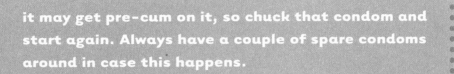

it may get pre-cum on it, so chuck that condom and start again. Always have a couple of spare condoms around in case this happens.

◎ Squeeze the tip, so the semen will have somewhere to go, then roll the condom down until it hits the base of the penis.

◎ If you're uncircumcised (more on this in chapter 3), you may want to roll back the foreskin before putting the condom on. This depends mainly on the size of the foreskin—you may have to experiment to find out what works best.

Once the condom is on, you're ready to have sex.

When you're done, it's important to remove and get rid of the condom the right way.

◎ Holding the base of the condom so it doesn't fall off, pull the penis out of your partner.

◎ Keeping your penis away from your partner, carefully remove the condom so no fluid spills out. Don't grab the condom from the tip and try to whip it off. This might cause semen to go flying across the room.

> ◎ **After checking for rips or tears, tie the condom in a knot and chuck it. Throw it in a garbage pail—condoms tend to clog up toilets and can reappear when someone other than you or your partner has to pee.**

If you discover that a condom has broken or torn during sex, or if the condom stays inside the vagina or anus after sex, you and your partner may be at risk for STDs. If you're female, and the condom was your only form of birth control, you may also need to think about emergency contraception (see chapter 6).

Most condoms you find in the drug store are made of latex. But if you or your partner is allergic to latex, polyurethane condoms are a great alternative (Trojan and Durex are two well-known brands that make polyurethane condoms). Some say they feel better than latex condoms because they transmit more body heat.

There are also some condoms that are made of lambskin. *Lambskin condoms protect only against pregnancy; the HIV virus and other STDs can still get through those condoms.*

A few other important things you should know about condoms:

Lubricant: Lubricant keeps condoms from tearing—many condoms come with lubricant already on them, and you can always buy extra separately. Some lubes contain spermicide, and some don't—only use one with spermicide if pregnancy is a concern (see chapter 6 for more information on spermicide). With latex condoms, always use a water-based lubricant—anything with oil in it (such Vaseline, baby oil, cooking oil, or hand lotion) could damage the condom. (Don't believe me? Blow a condom up like a balloon and rub baby oil on it. See how long it takes for the condom to pop.) Water-based lubricants are sold in drug stores and anywhere you can buy condoms.

Size: If the condom doesn't roll down easily, it's too small. If it doesn't fit snugly, it's too big. Condoms come in many different sizes. Make sure you're wearing the right size, so it doesn't tear or come off during sex.

Storage: Condoms should be stored in a cool place and should not be subjected to temperature changes. It's okay to put a condom in a wallet before going out, but you shouldn't permanently store it there. Try carrying them in a reinforced pocket of your backpack or bag. Some manufacturers also make condom wallets or key-chain condom holders that will provide more protection, and some condom brands even come in their own travel packaging—round plastic or metal cylinders. To check out various condom brands and products, go to www.condomania.com. And remember, if the packaging has been damaged or the expiration date has passed, don't use it!

Oral sex: Most people don't love the idea of using a condom for a blow job, but it's the only protection there is. You can use a flavored condom or a flavored lube—that's what they're for—and you can use one that's a little too big and put some lube inside as well, to give him a little more sensation. (For anal and vaginal sex, always use a snug-fitting, nonflavored condom.) If you don't use a condom, you can lower your risk to some degree by making sure your partner doesn't ejaculate in your mouth, but there are no guarantees that will prevent an STD.

The Female Condom

The female condom is an alternative to the more popular male one. This is a tube of polyurethane with two flexible rings—an inner ring and an outer ring. The inner ring goes all the way inside the vagina and rests against the cervix. To insert it, squeeze the sides of the inner ring together and put it as far inside the vagina as it will go—it's a lot like putting in a tampon.

The walls of the vagina should hold it in place. The other ring stays outside the vagina; the penis should go through this ring—make sure it doesn't get pushed inside the vagina during sex. Afterward, reach inside and squeeze the sides of the inner ring together to take it out.

The female condom can take a little getting used to, but since you can insert it way in advance you don't have to fumble with it under pressure. Some guys find it more pleasurable than the male condom. On the other hand, some say it makes funny noises during sex—this can be a pro or a con depending on your sense of humor.

Dental Dams

A dental dam is a square of latex (the same material most condoms are made out of) that you can put over the vulva for oral sex on a girl. They make these in flavors, just like condoms. You can buy dental dams at some sex stores, but if you don't have one handy, you can cut down the side of a condom to make one. You can also use plastic wrap as a substitute for a dental dam, but NOT as a substitute for a condom.

Make sure you don't flip the dental dam over at any point while you're using it—in other words, your mouth should only touch one side of it the whole time. Some of them are marked so you don't get confused; if they're not, you can use a permanent magic marker to indicate which side is which.

Just like with condoms, using a dental dam will be more pleasurable with a little lubricant. It might take a little while to get the hang of using one, but I'm sure your partner won't mind if you spend a lot of time practicing.

QUESTIONS

I want to use condoms, but whenever I go to put one on, I lose my erection. What do I do?

This happens to guys of all ages, particularly when they don't have much experience with sex or condoms. Practice will help. Asking your partner to put the condom on for you might help too—having them touch you might be a little sexier than doing it yourself. Whatever you do, resist the urge to chuck the condom over your shoulder "just this once," or to start having sex and put the condom on later. You're using a condom for good reasons; don't give up just because it's not working right away. It will get better, and in the meantime, there are other ways for you and your partner to enjoy yourselves until you can get the condom situation worked out.

My partner and I haven't been having safer sex, but I've been hearing so much about STDs, I think we should start. How do I bring this up?

I applaud you for wanting to start making sex safer for both you and your partner. This may not be an easy subject to talk about, but if you feel the need to put some latex between you, then you should go with your gut.

How this conversation will go depends on what kind of relationship you have with your partner. If you have agreed to have sex only with each other, you may be worried he'll think you're cheating or think you're accusing *him* of cheating. No matter what your relationship is like, he may feel a little bit defensive. Be prepared for this. Let him know that safer sex is a way to take responsibility for your health and his.

Think carefully about *why* you want to start having safer sex. Let your partner know what you've learned about STDs and why you've made the decision to start being safer. If it helps, show her this chapter, so she'll have a chance to learn more about STDs too.

6 Planning, Not Parenthood: Birth Control

. . . .

HOW DOES A WOMAN GET PREGNANT?

A WOMAN GETS PREGNANT WHEN A SPERM, WHICH COMES OUT OF THE man's penis, meets an egg, which is in the woman's body. Women have hundreds of eggs in their ovaries, and every month one of those eggs pops out of an ovary and comes down the fallopian tube. This is called ovulation. If, while the egg is traveling, it meets a sperm, that sperm might fertilize the egg (usually in the fallopian tube). After that happens, the egg and sperm travel together the rest of the way down the fallopian tube to the uterus. If the egg implants in the wall of the uterus, the woman is officially pregnant. The egg stays there and grows for nine months into a baby.

That's how you *do* get pregnant. But this chapter will help make sure you *don't* get pregnant until you're good and ready.

How Do I Choose the Best Birth Control Method for Me?

There are a few questions to ask yourself when choosing a form of birth control:

How Easy Will It Be to Get This Method?

Hormonal methods, diaphragms, and cervical caps require a visit to a doctor before you can use them. Condoms, on the other hand, are available at virtually every drug store. Which method you choose may depend on what you feel comfortable going out and getting. If you're not mature enough to do what it takes to purchase a method of birth control (whether that means buying condoms at your local drug store, where you may run into someone you know, or talking to a doctor about a diaphragm), then you're probably not mature enough for the responsibilities that come with being sexually active.

What Method Can I Get Without My Parents Knowing?

If you feel you can talk to your parents openly about sex, that's great, and I recommend you do so. However, you have the right to privacy when it comes to your sexual health. If you don't want to discuss your sex life with your parents, you and/or your partner will need to be able to afford whatever method you choose. Condoms are relatively cheap, while the pill requires a regular monthly expense (and it may be difficult to get it covered by your health insurance without your parents knowing). If you want a method that requires a prescription, talk to your doctor (ask about their confidentiality policy first) or go to an adolescent health clinic or your local Planned Parenthood. Some of these places are inexpensive or free for teens, so you may be able to afford it without help from your parents.

What Can I Afford?

Will hormonal methods or a diaphragm be covered by your health insurance plan? Does your school or health center give out free condoms?

Do I Also Want Protection Against Sexually Transmitted Diseases?

The condom and the female condom are the only methods that protect against STDs (and they do that very well) in addition to pregnancy. If you are having sex with someone who has had previous partners, or may currently have other partners, look no further. Protecting against STDs is every bit as important as protecting against unwanted pregnancy (see chapter 5 for more information).

How Will My Body Respond to Hormones?

Hormonal methods of birth control may have side effects, and sometimes the only way to know how such methods will affect your body is to try using one. On the other hand, some hormonal methods have very helpful side effects—they have been known to make periods more regular, eliminate nasty menstrual cramps, and even clear up acne. Talk to your doctor about the best method for you. He or she can talk to you more about your options—for example, there are many different brands of the birth control pill, and he or she can help you choose which one is right for you. If you smoke, most hormonal methods will not be safe for you to use. If you don't like the idea of using hormones, or if your body doesn't respond well to them, you should consider barrier methods instead.

How Responsible Am I/How Responsible Is My Partner?

Guys, do you feel confident your girlfriend will take the pill every day? Can you help her out by reminding her? If remembering something every day is too hard, consider a method that only requires remembering once a week (the ring, the patch) or even less often (the shot). If you choose to use condoms, will you be able to reliably use them every time?

How Easy Will It Be for Me to Use This Method?

Putting in a diaphragm or the inner ring of a female condom might take practice. If this is too hard, you might want to try another method.

Note: It's great to use two methods for double protection—for example, use a condom for protection against STDs, and a diaphragm or a hormonal method for extra protection against pregnancy. However, DO NOT use two condoms at the same time, or the male and female condom together. That will just make it more likely they'll both tear. Instead, use one, and use it right!

BIRTH CONTROL METHODS

The most widely used forms of birth control are barrier methods and hormonal methods.

Barrier Methods

A barrier method is anything that blocks the sperm from meeting the egg.

The Condom

The most popular barrier method around, this is a device, usually made of latex, that covers the penis during intercourse.

How to use it: See chapter 5 for instructions.

How well does it work? Condoms protect against pregnancy 97 percent of the time when you account for human error. If you use them right every single time (following all the instructions in chapter 5 or in the package) they can be as much as 99 percent effective.

How do I get it? Available at your local drug store, they cost less than a dollar each and are cheaper if you buy a bigger box.

Pros They are cheap and easy to use.

Cons The guy can't put one on until his penis is hard, so you have to stop in the middle of things to put it on.

The Female Condom

This is a type of condom that goes into the vagina rather than on the penis. It's made out of polyurethane rather than latex.

How to use it See chapter 5 for instructions.

How well does it work? It works about 95 percent of the time.

How do I get it? Available at some drug stores and health clinics, they cost about $2.50 each.

Pros Some guys say they feel better than male condoms.

Cons They can be hard to put in, and some people say they make a lot of noise during sex!

Note: The condom and female condom are the only methods of birth control that protect against STDs as well as pregnancy.

Spermicide

A foam, cream, jelly, film, or suppository that contains nonoxynol-9, a chemical ingredient that kills sperm. Some condoms come with a spermicidal lubricant already on them, so you get added protection without doing anything extra.

How to use it Following the package directions, insert the spermicide into the vagina shortly before having sex.

How well does it work? It's best when used along with a condom or female condom; when used alone, it's only about 75 to 80 percent effective.

How do I get it? Available at your local drug store, it costs between $4 and $8 for foam or gel applicator kits, film, or suppositories (something you insert into the vagina, where it melts).

Pros It can provide extra lubrication and extra protection when used with a condom.

Cons When used a lot, it may increase the risk of STDs by irritating the inside of the vagina or anus. It's recommended during vaginal sex, when pregnancy is a concern, but for anal sex, be sure to use lubricants that don't contain nonoxynol-9.

Diaphragms or Cervical Caps

A little cup, which you fill with spermicidal foam or jelly before you put it in, that rests against the cervix. To insert, squeeze the sides together and slide it inside the vagina until it rests against your cervix.

How well do they work? 85 to 95 percent effective.

How do I get it? You must visit your gynecologist to be fitted for a diaphragm or cervical cap, and you must be refitted if you gain or lose more than ten pounds. They can cost between $15 and $75 (though unlike with other barrier methods, this is a one-time cost). Your health insurance may cover these methods.

Pros You can put it in several hours before you have sex, so you don't have to interrupt anything.

Cons You have to be comfortable sticking something in your vagina to use it, and it provides no protection against STDs.

The Sponge

A foam device that is inserted into the vagina before sex that prevents pregnancy by covering the cervix and by releasing spermicide.

How to use it Moisten the sponge with water and push it gently into the vagina until it rests against the cervix. (Read the package for more specific instructions on how to insert it.)

How well does it work? It's 90 percent effective when used properly by girls who have never given birth.

How do I get it? Available at most drug stores, sponges cost $8 to $9 for a package of three.

Pros Can be inserted hours before you have sex, so you don't have to interrupt anything, and can be worn up to thirty hours afterward. You can have sex with the same sponge for up to twenty-four hours (though once you take it out you must throw it away).

Cons Should not be used during your period or if you have an infection. Some people have a difficult time inserting it, and it does not prevent against any STDs.

Hormonal Methods

A hormonal method contains hormones that affect a woman's ability to get pregnant (at the moment, there are no hormonal methods for men). The hormones in these methods usually prevent ovulation (described in chapter 2). In addition, they make the mucus around the cervix thicker to keep sperm from being able to get to an egg, and they change the lining of the uterus to make it less likely that a fertilized egg could implant there. You need a doctor to prescribe any of these methods.

You can take these hormones in a variety of forms.

The Pill

The most common hormonal method; it's taken once a day.

The Patch

Sort of like a big Band-Aid that you can wear on your arm, butt, or stomach. You wear one patch each week for three weeks, then take one week off and start again.

The NuvaRing

A rubber ring that is inserted into the vagina and rests against the cervix, just like a diaphragm or cervical cap. You wear one for three weeks, take it out for the fourth week, then start again the next week.

Depo Provera (aka "The Shot")

An injection you get from a doctor every three months.

How well do they work? If used consistently, hormonal methods are 99 percent effective.

How do I get them? You must get a prescription from your doctor for these methods. The cost varies depending on the method. Your health insurance may cover some of the cost.

Pros They're very easy to use, and you don't have to interrupt sex to use them as you do with lots of barrier methods.

Cons You may experience side effects, such as nausea, weight gain, bleeding between periods, and a reduced sex drive. Also, hormonal methods provide no protection against STDs.

Note: It's never okay to use a friend's birth control. While hormonal methods are usually safe, there are some health issues that would prevent a doctor from prescribing them to you. You should only use a method that your doctor has approved for you.

Methods That Are *Not* Recommended for Teens

IUD (Intrauterine Device)

A small plastic device, which a doctor inserts into your uterus, that contains hormones or copper to keep sperm from fertilizing an egg. This method is not recommended for a female who has not yet had children, as her uterus may not be able to hold an IUD.

Vasectomy

The male's vas deferens is cut and tied so sperm will no longer be able to leave the body.

Tubal Ligation

The female's fallopian tubes are cut so eggs will not be able to travel to the uterus.

Note: Because vasectomy and tubal ligation are intended to prevent pregnancy permanently, they are not recommended for people under the age of thirty who have not yet had children.

Natural Family Planning

Some couples, rather than using any of the above methods, choose to monitor a woman's menstrual cycle and avoid sex on the days when she is most likely to get pregnant. A woman can keep track of her fertility by observing her body in a variety of ways—she can look at changes in her body temperature (using a special basal body thermometer), changes in the discharge from her vagina (the consistency of her discharge changes with the time of the month), and keep track of her menstrual periods on a calendar. These methods are *not* recommended for teenagers. They require a long-term commitment—women often keep records of their menstrual cycles for as long as six months before relying on this method. In addition, they only work with women who have very regular menstrual cycles, which is rarely the case for teenagers. The truth is, these methods work best for couples who are *trying* to get pregnant and are keeping track of the best times of the month to have sex for that reason.

MYTHS ABOUT PREGNANCY

Myth: She can't get pregnant if he pulls out.

Withdrawal (pulling out before the guy ejaculates) is *not* a reliable method of birth control. First of all, some guys pre-ejaculate—a little bit of clear fluid comes out from the end of the penis—before they ejaculate. That fluid can contain enough sperm to get the girl pregnant. Second, a guy can't always be sure of when he's going to ejaculate—sometimes it takes him by surprise.

Myth: She can't get pregnant while she has her period.

In the introduction to this chapter, we looked at a woman's menstrual cycle and discussed the most likely time of the month for her to get pregnant— about halfway between one period and the next. During her period she's less likely to get pregnant. But here's the catch: While some girls have very regular cycles (there are always the same number of days between periods), lots of girls don't, and the younger a girl is, the less likely it is that her periods are regular and predictable. The truth is, you can never be sure it's completely safe to have sex without a condom or some other kind of birth control. Your best bet is to find the method that works best for both of you and use it all the time.

Myth: She can't get pregnant if it's her first time having sex.

She can get pregnant whether it's her first time or her last.

Myth: She can't get pregnant if he smokes marijuana.

While there is some evidence that smoking pot may affect a guy's sperm count, this does not mean that if a guy smokes pot—even a lot of it—he can't get someone pregnant.

Myth: She can't get pregnant if she has sex standing up.

She can get pregnant no matter what position you do it in.

WHAT IF THE CONDOM BROKE . . . ?

Another myth I've heard: If a condom tears, or after unprotected sex, a girl can prevent pregnancy by douching, jumping up and down, or drinking various substances. The truth is, there is only one safe way to prevent pregnancy *after* having unprotected sex. Whether she has sex against her will, the condom breaks, or she just plain forgets, she has a backup option: emergency contraception (also known as Plan B or the "morning after pill").

Emergency contraception is available at pharmacies without a prescription to men and women over the age of eighteen (proof of age is required). Girls under eighteen should call 1-888-NOT-2-LATE, the nearest

Planned Parenthood, or a doctor or pharmacist to get a prescription. (Pharmacists will not give E.C. to boys under eighteen.)

Emergency contraception isn't the same thing as the abortion pill (discussed at the end of this chapter). It's a pill she can take after sex, but before she gets pregnant, to make sure she *doesn't* get pregnant. Even after a girl has sex, it's not too late to prevent her from dropping an egg, or to prevent an egg from getting fertilized. That's what the morning-after pill does.

In order for emergency contraception to be effective, it's recommended that she take it no later than ninety-six hours after she has unprotected sex, and the sooner the better (within seventy-two hours is best). She may feel some side effects, like an upset stomach, but they're usually not too bad. A provider will explain the risks and side effects to her in detail.

While it's great to have the choice of taking emergency contraception in situations like this, the morning-after pill should *not* be used as a form of birth control. If you need emergency contraception because you failed to use birth control, you may want to think about finding a new method, one that works for both of you and one you can use consistently. They call it Plan B because there should always be a Plan A.

IF YOU ARE PREGNANT . . .

Once you find out you're pregnant, you have three options: You can continue with the pregnancy and keep the child, you can give the child up for adoption, or you can have an abortion.

The first thing I recommend is talking to someone you trust. This can be a very difficult decision to make alone. Talk to a parent, a teacher, a doctor, or some other adult who can help you. If you have the support of the baby's father, ask him to come with you, or suggest that he talk to someone as well.

You should also see a doctor immediately. If you're not ready to make the decision quite yet (and you will need to make it soon), you should make sure the baby is healthy and that you're taking proper care of your body until you do make a decision.

If you don't have a regular doctor and are looking for a clinic, try visiting your local Planned Parenthood or adolescent health center. Wherever you go, if anyone on staff tries to pressure you to choose a certain option before you're ready, leave immediately and find someone else to help you (check out the resource section at the end of this book for some options). This is *your* choice. You should make it with the support of people who care about you, but in the end no one has the right to tell you what to do with your body.

Adoption

A girl who gives birth to a baby she cannot care for can give the baby up for adoption. She can see her local Planned Parenthood or check out www.adoption.com for information on how to do that.

If she feels she has no other choice, most states have laws that allow new mothers to safely and legally leave unwanted infants at certain locations. Each state is different in terms of how young the infant has to be (the range is from three days to a year) and where they can be left (usually emergency rooms and fire stations). In some states this service is anonymous, while in other states the people receiving the baby are required to ask questions about the baby's medical history. The Guttmacher Institute has a list of the laws in each state at www.guttmacher.org/statecenter/spibs/spib_IA.pdf.

Abortion

Most abortions in the United States are done in the first trimester—that is, the first three months—of pregnancy. The sooner they are done, the easier they are. Most are done by a procedure called "vacuum aspiration." The doctor usually gives the woman a local anesthesia, meaning she is awake but her pelvic area is numbed. He or she opens up the woman's cervix—remember, that's the opening to the uterus, where the baby comes out during birth. Then the doctor inserts a tube into the cervix, and the tissue inside is sucked out. The woman can go home the same day.

This procedure is done up to the tenth week of pregnancy. If you're further along than that, a different method will be used. Your provider should answer all your questions about which method is most appropriate.

Another option for an early abortion is RU-486, the abortion pill, which can be used up to the ninth week of pregnancy. Rather than having a doctor remove the contents of the uterus, this medication makes the woman's uterus contract and release the tissue inside. The woman will experience bleeding and maybe some cramping—some people say it's like having a heavy period. She would have to return to the doctor in a few days to make sure the abortion is complete. RU-486 is almost always successful, but if for some reason it doesn't end the pregnancy successfully, the doctor would have to follow up by performing a surgical abortion.

It's best to talk to a health care provider about which option is right for you. As long as your abortion is done safely by a medical professional, it is very rare for it to affect your ability to get pregnant in the future, so if someday you do want to have a child, you will have that option.

In some states, if you're under the age of eighteen, you need your parents' permission to have an abortion. You can check out the Coalition for Positive Sexuality at www.positive.org/Resources/consent.html to find out the laws on parental notification for your state. Even if you live in a state that requires you to get your parents' permission, you have the right to go to court and ask a judge to hear your case and drop this requirement if you feel you cannot tell them.

Make sure you have someone to be with you on the day of the abortion, and plenty of support afterward. Having an abortion can bring up lots of different feelings, and it's important to make sure you can talk to someone about how you're doing.

QUESTIONS

I'm about to start using the birth control pill. How soon will it begin to work? Once I'm on it, can I stop using condoms?

The answer to this question depends on what kind of schedule your doctor has put you on. Depending on when your start date falls in your menstrual cycle, the pill may begin working right away, or you may need to wait a week before having unprotected sex. For the best advice, you should ask the doctor who prescribes the pill. If you want to play it safe, use a condom for the first month you are on the pill.

And remember, while the pill is great for protecting against pregnancy, it does not protect you against STDs. Before you choose to have sex without a condom, have an honest talk with your partner about sexual history and whether you plan to have sex only with each other. You might also consider getting STD tests for both of you.

Can you get pregnant from oral or anal sex?

The only way to get pregnant is for semen to get into the uterus. It's not possible to get pregnant from oral sex—if you swallow semen it can't get into the uterus from the stomach. It's also very rare to get pregnant from anal sex, though it is possible if semen drips out of the anus and into the vagina.

Is it possible to be pregnant and still get your period?

Yes. While menstruation usually stops when pregnancy begins, sometimes it continues for several months into the pregnancy. This can be confusing, because most girls assume that getting their period means they're *not* pregnant. Pay attention to your body, and if you're concerned about pregnancy, take a test even if you're still getting your period.

I skipped my period. Does that mean I'm pregnant?

It's possible—a missed period can often be the first sign of a pregnancy. However, your cycle could be irregular for lots of reasons other than pregnancy. The way to know for sure if you're pregnant is to take a test. Home pregnancy tests are very reliable, and they can tell you if you're pregnant as early as the day when you should be getting your period. For the best results, though, I recommend that you go to your doctor, an adolescent health center, or your local Planned Parenthood. That way you can be absolutely sure you'll get an accurate result, and there will be someone there to offer counseling if you truly are pregnant.

I'm a teenager and I *want* to have a baby. I feel a baby will give me someone to love. Can you give me any advice?

Having a baby is a huge responsibility that is very difficult for a young person. It can be incredibly rewarding, but it also takes a tremendous amount of time and energy. It means making a lot of compromises and putting someone else's needs before your own. You're still a kid—being a parent would make it much less likely that you'd be able to finish school and do your own growing up before you start taking care of someone else.

Before you make this decision, talk to an adult who can give you a clear picture of what your life would be like with a baby. In addition, if you know anyone around your age who has had a child, talk to them about what it has been like. Even better, if possible, volunteer to babysit for an infant for a full day with no pay (parents don't get paid for taking care of their children). You will get a sense of what it's like to be responsible for a baby full-time. Most teens who have kids at a young age wish, despite loving their child very much, that they had waited until they were a little older.

What if a pharmacist refuses to fill my birth control or emergency contraception prescription?

Some pharmacists refuse to fill prescriptions for birth control or emergency contraception for religious reasons. Some of the larger pharmacy chains are allowing this or are refusing to stock the products altogether. If you have this experience, find another pharmacist at that store or another pharmacy that *will* fill your prescription. If you're on the pill and you're using health insurance to pay for it, see if your insurance plan has a mail-order option. And if you disagree with pharmacists who refuse to fill prescriptions, exercise your power as a consumer: Let that pharmacy know they no longer have your business, and tell other people you know not to go there anymore.

If you want more information on this issue and on how to get your health insurance to cover your pills, go to www.covermypills.org.

Doing It Right

IN CHAPTER 4 WE TALKED ABOUT THE DECISION TO HAVE SEX, AND in chapters 5 and 6 I discussed how to prevent against unwanted pregnancy and sexually transmitted diseases. But those probably aren't the only kinds of questions you have. You may be wondering how it will feel for you and your partner, or you may have questions that seem too embarrassing to ask. Some of those are addressed in this chapter.

MUTUAL MASTURBATION

Mutual masturbation means touching each other's genitals with your hand—it's like masturbation, except you're doing it to someone else. Just like doing it by yourself, it's a great way for you and your partners to have orgasms without any risks. It can be a part of foreplay (kissing and touching that happens before intercourse to get your bodies aroused and ready for sex), or it can be the only thing you do. It's a great way to make each other feel good without all the responsibility and intensity that comes with penetrative sex.

ORAL SEX

Oral sex means touching someone's genitals with your mouth. Some people choose to have oral sex because they feel it's "not really sex." But make no mistake—oral sex can put you and your partner at risk for STDs, and it's an extremely intimate act. Think about it—do you want just anyone's face down there?

Girls often ask me if it's okay to swallow when they go down on a guy. The danger in swallowing after oral sex is that it may put you at risk for contracting certain STDs. (See chapter 5 for information on how to protect yourself during oral sex.) If you feel confident you don't need to be concerned about STDs, and if you *want* to swallow, it's okay to do it.

One last word about oral sex: If you want to get it, you should be willing to give it.

QUESTION

If I go down on someone, what will it taste like?

It's hard to describe how sexual fluids taste and smell, because it's so subjective—everyone smells and tastes different, and everyone *perceives* tastes and smells differently. That said, semen can taste salty, bitter, or a little like bleach, and it may smell a little like mushrooms. Vaginal secretions have been described as sweet, pungent, musky, metallic, or salty.

Some foods are said to make semen and vaginal fluids taste better—namely, fruits like pineapple, kiwi, and melon can make the taste a little less intense. Garlic, onion, and spicy foods may make a person taste bitter. And some say vegetarians taste yummier than meat-eaters. But the bottom line is, everyone tastes different—the only way to find out if foods have any effect is to run your own experiments.

SEX AND THE VAGINA

Vaginal sex involves a penis (or something resembling one) inside the vagina. For a girl, her first time doing this may be painful, especially if her hymen is still intact (see "popping the cherry" in chapter 12 for more information on that). She may experience some discomfort, and she may bleed a little bit—both of these things are normal.

If you're having vaginal sex for the first time, the best things to do are go slowly and communicate with your partner. It may seem embarrassing, but if you're close enough to have sex, you're close enough to talk about it. You'll need to let each other know what feels good and what doesn't as you're getting used to each other and to the experience of sex. You might want to start with a finger or two inside the vagina first, in order to take things slowly, and make sure you use plenty of lubricant.

Because vaginal sex involves so much friction, sometimes a girl might be a little sore and irritated afterward. It may even burn a little when she pees. If this only lasts for a short while after sex, and if it's not very painful, then it's nothing to worry about. If it burns a lot, or if it lasts for more than a couple of hours afterward, it could be a sign of an STD, so be sure to see a doctor.

QUESTION

Is it okay to have sex while I have my period?

Absolutely! Some people don't like having sex during menstruation, and others love it. As long as you and your partner both want to, it's okay to have sex at any time of the month. If your partner is a guy, his penis won't shrivel up and fall off. The only thing you might ruin is your sheets, so you might want to put a towel under you.

Many people believe you can't get pregnant while you have your period. As I discuss in chapter 6, it's possible to get pregnant at any time of the month, so you should always use birth control. And in fact, while you're menstruating, your body is even more vulnerable to STDs, so this is an especially bad time to go without a condom.

SEX AND THE PENIS

Lots of guys having vaginal or anal sex for the first time have trouble keeping an erection. There could be a lot of reasons for this. Most men have trouble staying hard at some point in their life. For a young guy having one of his first few sexual experiences, the most likely reason is that he has the jitters. Try not to sweat it when you lose an erection—it can be embarrassing, but the more you think about it, the worse the problem gets. Instead, remember that there are other ways you can both enjoy yourselves even if your penis isn't cooperating. Try to make light of the situation, move on, and if it really is that you're just nervous, you'll be able to stay hard when you get a bit more comfortable with yourself and your partner. If the problem persists, see a doctor.

Guys sometimes put something around the base of their penis—like a metal ring or a leather strap—to keep an erection longer. However, this is potentially dangerous. When you are sexually aroused, blood rushes to your genitals. If you keep the blood there artificially for too long, it can be dangerous and might cause blood clotting. Sometimes the experience of being aroused can be distracting and can cause a person to pay less attention to pain and discomfort that signals the body is in danger.

Although I recommend against it, if you feel you must experiment with such things, I urge you to be very careful and not to use something that traps the blood in your penis for more than twenty minutes.

If you're concerned that your erection is not lasting long enough during sexual activity, there are other ways to deal with this. If you are newly sexually active, know that you will last longer as you become more accustomed to having sex. If this is something that concerns you, try talking to a doctor or someone else you trust about it. And a lot of guys find that condoms help them last longer—how's that for a great reason to have safer sex?

Both pee and semen come out of the urethra, so can a guy accidentally pee during sex?

When a guy gets turned on and has an erection, the valve between the urethra and his bladder closes, so he won't pee during sexual activity.

ANAL SEX

Anal sex involves a penis (or something resembling one) inside the anus. This feels good for the person whose butt is getting penetrated because there are nerve endings in the anus, and it feels pleasurable to have them stimulated. If you don't believe me, the next time you poop, think about it. It feels kind of good. In addition, anal sex may feel good because it can stimulate the G-spot in females and the prostate in males (more about this in chapter 13).

Lots of people think about their butt as a one-way street. So it can be difficult to get used to something going in there rather than out. However, the anus can stretch. Just keep in mind that it's not as elastic as the vagina and can tear more easily.

You might want to give your body a chance to get used to anal sex by starting with something smaller, like a finger or two, or a sex toy designed for the anus. Just be careful: Any sex toy you put in your butt should be flared at the end so that it doesn't get lost in there.

And as always, the more lube the better. Since pregnancy isn't an issue here, you should use a lubricant that doesn't contain spermicide.

Remember that STDs can be transmitted through anal sex, so be safe (see chapter 5 for more information). And anything that touches your butt shouldn't then touch anyone's vulva or mouth before being washed carefully to avoid transferring bacteria from the anus. If you're using a condom for anal sex, you should take it off and put on a new one before that penis goes anywhere else.

QUESTION

If a guy likes it when you touch his anus, does that mean he's gay?

You can read more about sexual orientation in chapter 8. But the simple answer to this question is no. As I said above, anal stimulation can feel good for anyone—male or female, gay or straight—because of nerve endings in that part of the body. Sexual orientation is not defined by what we like to do in bed, but by *who* we want to do it with.

THE FIRST TIME

If you're about to have sex for the first time, you might be feeling kind of nervous. What if you can't keep your erection? What if it hurts? What if you orgasm too fast? What if there's blood? There could be many embarrassing and mood-wrecking scenarios going through your head.

There are lots of movies and TV shows where someone has sex for the first time and it's romantic, beautiful, and perfect. Here's a secret: Real-life first times are rarely like that. They're more likely to be awkward, confusing, and uncomfortable. If it's partly wonderful and partly embarrassing, you're ahead of the game.

Hopefully you're having sex because you feel you're informed and ready (if not, go back to page one!), and your partner is too. In that case, the best you can do is avoid hoping it'll be perfect and be open to whatever happens. If it doesn't feel good, try something different. If there's a penis involved that doesn't stay erect, do something else for a while and try again later. If your hymen breaks and you bleed all over your new white sheets, realize that it wasn't so smart to have intercourse for the first time on your new white sheets (and when you're done, soak them in soap and cold water). Have a few spare condoms and/or dental dams around in case you need them. Above all, keep a sense of humor. This will be your first time, but I can almost guarantee it won't be your last.

8 LGBTQ . . . Which One R U?

AS YOU READ IN CHAPTER 1, SEXUAL ORIENTATION REFERS TO *which sex* a person is attracted to—males, females, or both. People who are attracted to members of the opposite sex are heterosexual, or straight. People who are attracted to members of the same sex are homosexual—they may prefer the term "gay," or women may prefer "lesbian." And people who are attracted to both men and women may identify as bisexual.

Sexual orientation is a difficult topic for some people, but as a society, we've come a long way in the past few decades in terms of our comfort with this issue. If you asked your parents, I bet they'd tell you it was rare for someone they knew as a teen to be openly gay. Until very recently it was rare to see a movie or TV show with a central character who was gay and comfortable with his or her sexuality. Although we still have a long way to go before gay and lesbian people experience complete acceptance and equal rights, you are growing up in a time when there's more support and information available for gay or questioning teens than ever before.

If you're straight, I hope what you read in this chapter answers your questions about sexual orientation so that you will be an informed and empathic peer for those in your school or community who are coming out or dealing with issues of sexual orientation. If you're gay, lesbian, bisexual, or questioning, I hope what you learn here will help answer your questions about your sexuality.

WHY ARE SOME PEOPLE GAY?

When people talk about sexual orientation, one question seems to come up a lot: Is it a choice? Experts agree that sexual orientation is something we're born with. It's not something we choose, and it's not something we can change. Over the years there have been programs designed to change people's sexual orientation—there are still some around today. But most people agree they just don't work.

If you're straight, think about this for a moment: When did you *decide* to be straight? Could you just as easily have chosen to be gay? Probably not. And the same goes for gay people.

What people *can* choose is whether or not to live as openly gay people. A gay person can decide to remain "in the closet"—to hide their sexuality, or live the life of a straight person and date or even marry members of the opposite sex. However, the only reason to do this is fear of being gay in a world that is not very accepting of homosexuality. Most people are happier when they don't have to hide anything from any-one—when they are honest about who they are.

Some people do make the choice to experiment with members of the same sex. You or someone you know may have had a sexual experience with a member of the same sex because you were curious about what it would be like. This too is something people can choose. But most people find that the attraction they feel for one sex or the other is not a matter of choice.

I know people who have spent some time having same-sex partners and who later went on to have opposite-sex partners. It just shows how complex and interesting sexuality can be. However, if someone tells you that they are gay, your best bet is to believe them until they tell you otherwise.

There seems to be some evidence that sexual orientation runs in families, though there's no solid proof that this is the case. There is some controversy around even trying to find out for sure exactly what causes some people to be gay. Some people say that if a "gay gene" is discovered, it will make a strong case against discrimination and convince people once and for all that being attracted to the same sex is not a choice. On the other hand, many in the gay community say that it shouldn't matter *why* someone is gay—everyone should be treated equally no matter whom they love and lust for. In any case, people will continue searching for answers to this question.

You may know someone who was sexually abused at a young age and went on to identify as gay or lesbian. The two are not related. Unfortunately, lots of people experience some kind of sexual abuse at a young age. Most of them turn out to be straight because most people in general are straight.

HOW DO I KNOW IF I'M GAY?

Some gay people say they knew they were gay from the time they were five or six years old. Others don't come to understand that they're gay until they're much older, some when they are already married to members of the opposite sex. There's no special time when people discover they're gay. However, since adolescence is a period when most people think a lot about sexuality in general, it's a time when lots of people come out to themselves and others about their sexual orientation.

It can sometimes be difficult for people to figure out their sexual orientation, in part because most people around them identify as heterosexual (straight), and assume that most other people are heterosexual as well. Think about it: When you were little, did you have any good friends of the opposite sex? If you did, maybe someone (your parents or other friends) teased you about having a girlfriend or boyfriend, or joked that you two would get married some day. You probably also had friends of the same sex, and it's likely no one made similar jokes about them. Most straight people don't have to "figure out" they're straight, because everyone assumes they are.

In a world in which we see images of straight people everywhere—in the movies, on TV, in books, and on the street—it can be hard to be comfortable with feelings of attraction to a member of the same sex. We come to feel that being straight is something that's expected of us.

Even if feelings of same-sex attraction are there, it can be a long time before people acknowledge them to themselves or others. I know gay people who now realize, looking back, that they were attracted to the same sex for years before they were ready to acknowledge those feelings to themselves or anyone else. They thought what they were feeling was wrong and should be kept a secret, or that it would go away eventually. Others figured out their sexual orientation quite easily.

If you're noticing that you have crushes on members of the same sex, you may be wondering what this means about your sexual orientation. You may be discovering that you're gay, or you may be realizing that there are some people you really like regardless of what sex they are—I know straight people who, as teens, developed crushes on friends or teachers of the same sex. That's the thing about being a teen—you're having new feelings, and it's not always easy to understand what they mean. If you can't figure it out right now, it'll become clear to you eventually as you get to know yourself better.

If you're confused about your sexual orientation, you're not alone. Lots of teens struggle with this question. And more important, this is a confusing time for everyone your age. Whether they're questioning their sexual orientation or some other aspect of their sexuality, everyone your age spends a little time feeling puzzled about sex.

COMING OUT

People who discover that they're gay will probably go through the process of coming out. That means they will choose to tell people—parents, other family members, friends—about their sexual orientation. But before they can do this, they have to come out to themselves. Some people deny these feelings because they're afraid of what it might mean for them to be gay—they might feel their life will be more difficult if they have to live as a member of a minority, and they might feel that they will disappoint or upset family or friends. For this reason, people may keep these feelings hidden for a long time. In the end, though, coming out can be a very free-ing experience for most people, because it means being able to stop hid-ing who they are.

If you're considering coming out, chances are you're thinking about how your friends and family members will react to this news. They may be surprised, or they may say they've known for a while and were just waiting till you were ready to tell them.

If possible, I suggest you start by coming out to someone you know you can trust to respond in a positive way. Hopefully he or she will sup-port you as you go through the process of coming out to others. If your school or community has an organization for Lesbian, Gay, Bisexual, Transgender, Questioning (LGBTQ) youth, you might try seeking out some support there. Or you might talk with a trusted friend or family member. If you know someone who is gay, try talking with them. You may also want to look at some websites that have information about what to expect when coming out: Parents and Friends of Lesbians and Gays (PFLAG), at www.pflag.org, and the Human Rights Campaign (www.HRC.org) are two sites that can give you more information.

You probably have some sense of how your parents will respond to your coming out. It's okay to choose *not* to come out to them if you are concerned about how they will react. Some people choose not to come out until they are no longer living with their parents and are financially independent. Others choose never to come out to their parents. This is a decision only you can make. If you do choose to come out to your family but are worried that they will become very upset or angry, try to arrange ahead of time for somewhere to stay for a few days if necessary. My hope is that this won't be something you'll need, but it's a good idea to be prepared.

Whenever you choose to come out, you may need to give your family members time to absorb the news. Especially if they don't have any idea you're gay, this may be a process rather than a one-time conversation. Not only are you telling them something about you that they might not know, but this might be the first time they've confronted the idea that you are a sexual being, a difficult thing for some parents to realize about their kid whether they're gay or straight. They'll probably have lots of questions, either right away or down the road. You can help them out by being armed with some good resources. If you find the PFLAG website helpful, you can start by sending them there—they can find information for families and perhaps find a chapter of this organization nearby.

You might also direct them to a book that will answer their questions about sexual orientation. I recommend *Is It a Choice?* by Eric Marcus. For younger members of your family, the same author has written *What if Someone I Know Is Gay?* Another suggestion: *The Family Heart: A Memoir of When Our Son Came Out,* by Robb Forman Dew. (You can find more resources in chapter 15.)

Sometimes I hear stories from people who came out to friends or family and were told they were just going through a phase and that they would snap out of it when they grew up or met the right person. When someone says that, it usually shows that he or she is uncomfortable learning that someone they care about is gay and prefer to think that it's temporary. However, most of the time when people come out, they're describing feelings that are probably not going to change.

The most important thing to remember when coming out to family members is to give them time and information. Be patient with them. Most of the time, when parents get upset about learning that their child is gay, it's because they are worried that their child's life is going to be harder than it would be if he or she were straight. They may be right—being gay means being a member of a minority and sometimes facing prejudice. You can help them by offering as much information as possible. And remind them that you're coming out to them because you want to have a close, honest relationship with them.

IS IT WRONG TO BE GAY?

Some people believe that it's wrong to be gay. They may say that males were simply meant to be with females and vice versa. But to say that it's wrong to be gay is to say that it's wrong for a person to be who they truly are and to love who they truly love. The bottom line is, sexual orientation is something we're born with and cannot change.

Many people believe that their religions declare homosexuality to be a sin. However, there are also people of all different faiths—including clergy members—who don't believe it's a sin. And for every person who can quote a passage from the Bible or some other religious text saying that homosexuality is wrong, there's someone else who can interpret that same passage to have a different meaning. Any piece of writing—whether it's the Bible or this book—can be interpreted in many different ways.

If you feel that homosexuality is sinful, ask yourself for a moment what your religion says about sex outside of marriage or sex for any reason other than to make babies. Ask yourself what your religion says about masturbation. Lots of religions teach that these things are sinful too, but many people find it easy to ignore these rules—perhaps because sex outside of marriage doesn't make most people half as uncomfortable as homosexuality does.

Most of the sinful things I can think of are harmful to other people. But being gay isn't harmful to anyone. Gay people, just like straight people, want to have loving relationships and want to have sex—they just want to do it with members of the same sex rather than members of the opposite sex. The bottom line is this: Although the teachings of any religion can be useful, they can never be a substitute for your ability to think for yourself about what is right or wrong.

In the past few years religious organizations have had a lot to say about homosexuality because gay people are fighting for the right to marry legally. However, this is not a religious issue. Gay people want to get married for the same reasons straight people do—because they want to make an official commitment to each other and take care of each other the same way straight couples do. Marriage gives couples legal rights: the right to make medical decisions in an emergency, the right to visit each other in the hospital, the right to inherit property when one of them dies, the right to adopt children together, and hundreds of other rights that straight couples take for granted. These rights aren't given to people by a church or a temple or a mosque. They are rights afforded to straight couples by the government. Gay couples simply want equal treatment under the law.

HOMOPHOBIA

Homophobia means fear or hatred of gay people. While lots of people might feel a little uncomfortable with homosexuality, being mean or prejudiced toward someone who is gay is really no different from being mean or prejudiced toward someone with a different race or religion from you—it's just plain wrong.

It's natural to feel a little confused by homosexuality, especially if you've never met someone who's gay or if you've been taught that being gay is wrong. Most people get over that pretty quickly once they get to know gay people. But some people can be very hateful toward those who are gay. Like with any other prejudice, there can be many reasons why. One reason is that such hateful attitudes are passed down from adults. Another reason is, the thought of being attracted to someone of the same sex is so scary to some people, they feel upset or disgusted thinking about *anyone* feeling that way.

BISEXUALITY

"Bisexual" is a term that describes people who feel attracted to both sexes—some even say that they are simply attracted to certain *people* regardless of their sex. For others, bisexual is the term that feels most comfortable during the transition into a gay identity.

Being bisexual does not mean a person can never be satisfied by just one partner. There are some people—gay, straight, or bisexual—who never seem satisfied with just one partner. But I don't think that's true of bisexual people in particular. If you think of any friend or partner you've ever had, he or she probably hasn't fulfilled every single one of your needs, because no one person can. That doesn't mean that a bisexual person can't fall in love with someone—of either sex—and feel satisfied in that relationship.

WHAT'S IN A NAME?

A student of mine once asked me why we have to have names for everything. Labels are meant to be descriptive, but sometimes they are more likely to make us feel boxed in. Rather than defining themselves as gay, straight, or bisexual, some people prefer the term "queer," which means their gender, sexual orientation, or sexuality in general falls outside the status quo. There are people who find this word offensive because it was originally used as a derogatory term, or because it is so inclusive that it lumps many different types of people into one group.

Lately teens are using more words than ever to define themselves—some I've heard recently include heteroflexible, flexual, bicurious, questioning, pansexual, and genderqueer.

I'M HERE, I'M QUEER, NOW WHAT DO I DO?

If you've figured out you're gay and have gone through the process of coming out, you might think about joining an organization in your school or community for gay youth. If your school doesn't have one, think about being the pioneer who starts one—if you're interested in seeing your school recognize and support gay and bisexual kids, chances are you're not the only one. One organization that can give you more information on this is the Gay, Lesbian, and Straight Education Network (www.glsen.org).

You may also want to meet other gay kids your age, whether it's because you're interested in dating or just having friends who are gay. Check out chapter 15 for organizations for gay youth, and see if you can find one in your community. These organizations also have websites where you can connect with other gay teens, but you must be very careful about meeting people online (see "Being Safe Online" in chapter 14 for more information).

QUESTIONS

How many gay people are there?

It's hard to know the answer to this question because so many people hide the fact that they are gay. In 2001 the Human Rights Campaign estimated that gay people make up roughly 5 percent of the population of the United States.

I've heard estimates that range from 2 or 3 percent to 10 percent of the population, though a bigger percentage of teens have had at least one same-sex encounter without identifying as gay.

Some people think there are more gay people now than there have been in the past. It's true that being gay *seems* like it is becoming more common. This is probably because we see more images of gay people in the media, and there are more people living openly gay lives. The truth is, the number of gay people probably isn't increasing; we are just seeing and hearing more about more gay people because our society is slowly becoming more accepting of them. So a gay person who might have hidden his or her sexual orientation twenty years ago is more likely to be living with a gay partner today.

How do gay people have sex?

As I mentioned in chapter 1, "sex" can mean different things to different people. Lots of people automatically assume sex means penis-in-vagina intercourse, but for gay people, it may mean oral or anal intercourse, or it may mean mutual masturbation (using hands to stimulate each other's genitals).

Can a girl have sex with another girl? If a girl only has sex with girls, will she always be a virgin?

Although lots of people define virginity by whether or not a person has had vaginal intercourse with a member of the opposite sex, this definition is not a great one, especially when it comes to gay people. If we define virginity that way, then gay people who have only been intimate with same-sex partners will always be virgins. Most of the adult gay people I know wouldn't feel right about calling themselves virgins—the word makes them sound like they aren't sexually experienced, which just isn't true.

A gay person may feel they lost their virginity the first time they had oral or anal sex. Or they might feel that the word "virgin" is not important or relevant to them.

If I have a sexual dream or fantasy about someone of the same sex, does that mean I'm gay?

Having a dream about someone of the same sex doesn't necessarily mean you're gay, and having a sexual dream about anyone—male or female—doesn't necessarily mean you want to get sexual with that person.

Dreams can have lots of meanings. They can represent desires, fears, or sometimes nothing at all. They can give you insight into feelings you might bury during the day. Plenty of people have dreams in which they're doing things they would never want to do in real life. And sometimes dreams are just your brain's way of filtering out the day's information.

When sex pops up in a dream, it's not always really about sex—sometimes sex is just a symbol of something else, like feelings of closeness or strong emotions. Lots of people ask me what it means when they dream about having sex with a sibling or parent. That kind of dream can be a little disconcerting, but it might be your brain's way of working out your feelings about your relationship with that person.

You may eventually decide that you like fantasizing about members of the same sex, but you don't actually want to act on those fantasies. Or you may decide that you want to explore these feelings with someone. There are many ways in which you can be attracted to someone. As time goes on your sexual orientation will become more clear to you.

I can tell you that it's normal for anyone—gay or straight—to have sexual fantasies or dreams about someone of the same sex. These fantasies could be a sign you're having feelings you will need to keep exploring, or it may be that you're a heterosexual person with a rich and interesting fantasy life.

I'm a guy and sometimes I like it when my girlfriend puts her finger in my butt. Does that mean I'm gay?

Sexual orientation is determined by *who* you want to have sex with, not by *what* you do with your sexual partners. You like it when your girlfriend touches your anus because you recognize that part of your body feels good when stimulated (see chapter 13 for more information). Congratulations—lots of people never get comfortable with that part of their bodies. Your sexual orientation only comes into the picture if you want a *guy* to touch your anus.

My friend told me he's gay. Does that mean he's attracted to me?

The only person who knows the answer to that is your friend. But what's more important is that he confided in you. If your friend hasn't come out to very many people yet, he may have told you because he trusts you and wants you to know what he's discovered about himself. If he has come out to lots of people, then he was probably telling you because he doesn't want to keep a big part of his identity a secret. Don't assume he's attracted to you, but do take his trust in you as a compliment. Chances are he likes you, but only he knows if his feelings are more than just friendly.

Boys Will Be Boys...or Will They? Transgender and Intersex

· ·

9

WHAT'S THE DIFFERENCE BETWEEN SEX AND GENDER?

IN CHAPTER 2, WE TALKED ABOUT BIOLOGICAL SEX—THE PHYSICAL characteristics of being male or female, which you're born with. Some people use the term gender to describe this, but, in fact, gender is something different—it's your presentation of yourself to the world as a guy or girl. While your sex has to do with who you are *physically*, your gender has to do with your *identity*.

If this sounds confusing, it's probably because most people's sex and gender match, and they don't think much about it. Most biological males identify as boys and men; most females, as girls and women. But this isn't always the case.

This chapter is about what happens when people feel that the gender that was assigned to them based on their sex is not the one they feel comfortable identifying with. In addition, at the end of this chapter I'll discuss what happens when a person's biological sex isn't clear because their genitals resemble both a male's and a female's.

In the introduction to chapter 8, I told you that our society has become much more accepting of gay and lesbian people in the past few decades. However, most people are less knowledgeable about—and less accepting of—transgender and intersex people. That's why I've included a chapter on this subject, even though the information here may directly apply to only a very few of my readers. If you're one of those readers, I hope this information is helpful. If you're not, you've probably taken for granted that sex and gender are relatively simple for you. That's not the case for everyone, and I hope what you learn here will be helpful if you know someone—now or down the line—who is transgender or intersex.

For starters, the terms transvestite, transgender, and transsexual confuse lots of people, so lets clear them up:

◎ **A transvestite is someone who likes to dress as the opposite sex because they find it sexually arousing, or for performance. Drag queens (men who dress up as women) and drag kings (women who dress up as men) are transvestites.**

◎ **Someone who is transgender feels that they do not identify with the gender they were raised with. In other words, someone who is biologically female identifies as a boy, or someone who is biologically male identifies as a girl. This person may or may not choose to live life as the gender they identify with.**

◎ **A transsexual is a transgender person who chooses to fully live as the sex they identify with. They may also choose to change their sex—a process that involves taking hormones and undergoing sex reassignment surgery.**

This doesn't mean that girls who are a little masculine or boys who are a little feminine are transgender. Most people identify with the gender they're assigned but exhibit some characteristics of the opposite gender. Transgender people, though, *identify* with a different gender than they were assigned. They may want to change their names, the pronouns people use in reference to them, etc.

It's also important to realize that a person's gender (whether they identify as a guy or as a girl) is different from their sexual orientation (whether they are *attracted* to guys or girls). If someone tells you they're transgender, don't make any assumptions about who they're attracted to—just like with a person whose gender *does* match their biological sex, a transgender person can be gay, straight, or bisexual. Lots of people don't understand this, which can make being transgender especially tricky.

HOW DO I KNOW IF I'M TRANSGENDER?

Most of us have some pretty rigid ideas about gender. People with vaginas are girls, and people with penises are boys, and there's no gray area. But you may be discovering that you don't fit comfortably into the gender you were assigned. You may feel you fit comfortably in the "opposite" gender, somewhere between the two, or in neither gender. If you're thinking the label of "boy" or "girl" that was assigned to you at birth doesn't match how you feel, you may be questioning your gender identity.

Coming Out and Transitioning

People who discover that they are transgender often go through a process similar to what someone might go through when they discover they're gay—they tell friends and family about their identity. And just like when someone comes out as being gay, this can sometimes be a difficult process. When a person has decided to live with their new gender identity, their parents may have an especially hard time adjusting to the fact that their son is now their daughter, or vice versa.

For some people, coming out to their family could mean facing a lot of anger. If you are concerned about your family's response, you may want to secure a place to stay for a short time while they absorb this information. Don't do anything that will put you at any risk. If you're not sure you're ready to come out to your family, find someone at school or in your community to talk to. (There are resources in chapter 15 that can help.)

If transgender people choose to live publicly as the gender they identify with, they may begin to **transition**. They may change their style of dress, their appearance, their name, and the pronouns (such as "him" or "her") they'd like people to use to identify them.

Medical transition means taking hormones and having surgery in order to fully transition one's sex. This is a big step, but some people feel it's very important that their identities and their bodies match, no matter what steps they must take to make this happen. In most states, people under the age of eighteen need a parent's permission for medical transition.

Medical transitions usually involve seeing a therapist and being diagnosed with gender identity disorder. People get diagnosed with this disorder if they have a very strong identity with the opposite gender of their sex—they either want to be that gender or insist they *are* that gender—and their assigned gender feels uncomfortable or downright wrong to them. The fact that this diagnosis is necessary to get a sex-change operation is controversial, because many transgender people prefer not to be labeled as having a disorder. However, because sex reassignment surgery is a very serious and irreversible preocedure, the medical profession requires that people get a professional diagnosis before undergoing this process.

doing it right

If you are transgender and feel it's important for you to medically transition, do so safely—meaning, with the supervision of a doctor. Taking hormones given to you by anyone other than a doctor can lead to very serious health risks. (If you are transgender and need help transitioning, you can find resources in chapter 15.)

Transitioning at School

Just as it can be tough to come out to close friends and family, living full-time with a new gender identity can be challenging for a student. If you've come out as transgender and want to transition at school, your first step is to talk to someone—a counselor, a trusted teacher, or a faculty member connected with your school's LGBTQ organization, if there is one. Find someone you can depend on to be your ally. You may need them to help you make some changes at your school. For example, you may need to discuss access to appropriate restrooms and locker rooms, and if your school has a dress code, you may need to explain that you will be wearing the clothing appropriate for your gender identity.

All of this will take time and patience. It may be easier if your school has made accommodations for transgender students before. However, it's more likely that they haven't. If the faculty members at your school are open-minded and willing to help, you will give them and your classmates an opportunity to learn a great deal about gender identity.

This will also be a chance to see just how open-minded your classmates are. My hope is that they embrace you and your new identity with open arms, but you are probably aware that this might not be the case. Transitioning can be not just difficult but downright dangerous for some students, depending on where they live and how sophisticated their classmates are. Your identity is of course tremendously important to you. Your personal safety and your ability to get an education in a comfortable environment, however, are also very important. You need to figure out what your priorities are, depending on the resources and support available and how strongly you feel. If transitioning is going to make life really difficult, it may be worth it to wait until it feels right—whether that means when you graduate from high school, when you're living on your own, when you're financially independent, or whenever you will be safe.

INTERSEX

Intersex is a term that refers to someone who was born with some of the characteristics of each sex—their genitals are something between a male's and a female's. Intersex people develop differently in the womb, because of some variation in their chromosomes or their hormones. It may sound strange if you have never heard of it before, but the truth is, this occurs in about one out of every two thousand births. And if you don't think you know anyone like this, keep in mind that you probably haven't seen the genitals of most people you know!

You may have heard the word "hermaphrodite" to describe this. This is an outdated term—a combination of Hermes and Aphrodite, a Greek god and goddess. The term technically means that a person is both fully male and fully female, which is physically impossible.

There can be lots of variations in intersex people's bodies. They may have both ovaries and testicles, or one ovary and one testicle. They may have something that looks somewhere between a small penis and a large clitoris.

It may not be clear to anyone, when an intersex person is born, whether they will identify as male or female. And it will definitely not be clear whether they will be *attracted* to males or females.

If you yourself are intersex, you're not alone. Here are a few things you should know:

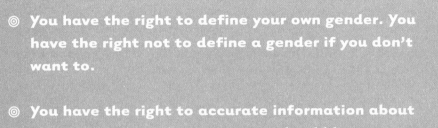

- ⦿ You have the right to define your own gender. You have the right not to define a gender if you don't want to.

- ⦿ You have the right to accurate information about your medical condition—no one should keep any information from you.

- ⦿ You should not be pressured by anyone to have surgery or take hormones unless you choose to.

- ⦿ If you want to connect with others who are intersex, there's a growing community all over the world. If possible, find a support group near you. There are support groups for parents of intersex kids as well.

To learn more about resources for intersex people, you can visit the Intersex Society of North America at www.isna.org or look for more resources in the last chapter of this book.

HOW DO TRANSGENDER AND INTERSEX PEOPLE HAVE SEX?

As a transgender friend of mine said when I asked him this question, they do "whatever feels right." How a transgender or intersex person defines sex is probably determined by a lot of things: what their genitals are like, what gender they identify as, and who they choose as partners. Just like with anyone else, sex is doing whatever feels good for both partners.

QUESTIONS

I have this friend who says she feels like a boy trapped in a girl's body. Should I call her "he" or "she"?

It sounds like your friend is transgender—someone who doesn't identify with the gender that matches their biological sex. However, the person who can best answer your question, and the question about the best pronouns to use, is your friend. My guess is that if you convey to your friend that you are not being judgmental but are just interested in learning more, you will make it clear you're asking because you're a supportive and respectful friend. However, keep in mind that your friend may be confused or still figuring this out as well.

I'm a guy, and I'm attracted to girls, but sometimes I feel like I want to *be* a girl. What should I do? Is there something wrong with me?

What you're experiencing may feel confusing, but you are not the only person to feel this way.

I highly recommend that you talk with someone you trust about how you're feeling—a parent, teacher, or a school counselor. Also, you might want to find out if your school or community has any services for transgender youth—more and more programs for gay, lesbian, and bisexual students are including transgender people under their umbrella.

Adolescence is a confusing time for everyone. It's a time when it's normal to question virtually everything about yourself. It's possible that these feelings are something you'll grow out of. It's also possible that they will become stronger and that you will grow into a transgender identity. Either way, keep in mind that you are still growing and changing and figuring yourself out—the fact that you don't know all the answers yet is normal.

If a girl is a tomboy, does that mean she's transgender?

The word "tomboy" is a pretty old-fashioned way to refer to a girl who is not traditionally "girly." A tomboy and a transgender person are two different things. The word "tomboy" describes a girl whose behaviors or mannerisms are considered by some to be boyish or masculine—this doesn't mean she thinks she's a boy or identifies as one; it just means she's not especially feminine. It also doesn't mean she's a lesbian. A person is transgender if they identify with a gender that does not match their sex.

I'm a guy, but I like to dress in women's clothing. Does that mean I'm transgender?

Some people like to dress in clothing of the opposite gender ("cross-dress," or dress in "drag") because it's something they find sexually arousing. They don't necessarily want to do so in public, and they don't want to change their gender. There may be something about women's clothing that just feels sexy to you, but this may have nothing to do with your gender identity.

Other people may start to cross-dress as a way of starting to come to terms with the feeling that they don't identify with the gender that matches their sex. So you may find women's clothing to be a turn-on, or you may want to *be* a woman. As you might have guessed, you're the only one who can figure out which one it is.

We have some pretty rigid ideas about what makes a girl a girl and what makes a guy a guy. We assume each gender should look and act and dress a certain way. When you meet someone who is transgender or intersex (or if you discover that *you* fit one of those descriptions), it can be confusing and uncomfortable, but ultimately, it can help you challenge those rigid ideas about how people "should" be. Everyone you know is different from you in some way, and while that may be hard to deal with at first, struggling to find comfort with it will make you a more open-minded person.

D.I.Y.: Masturbation

10

YOU'VE PROBABLY HEARD A LOT OF MYTHS ABOUT MASTURBATION—YOU may even believe some of them are true. So let me start by telling you what masturbation will NOT do. It will *not* stunt your growth, affect your period, speed up or slow down puberty, increase or decrease your penis size, lower your sperm count, or affect breast development. You will not go blind, and you will not get hairy palms. And when you go to the doctor, he or she will not be able to tell that you masturbate. The bottom line is that masturbation is a healthy, normal sexual activity.

In fact, masturbation is one of the safest ways to experience sexual pleasure. Some reasons why:

◎ **Masturbation can't get you pregnant or give you an STD.**

◎ **It's a terrific way to find out more about your body— to learn where and how you like to be touched.**

◎ **If you do it with a partner at your side, it's a great way to teach them what you like as well.**

◎ **You don't need anyone's consent but your own!**

According to some statistics, most boys and at least half of girls have masturbated at least once by the time they're eighteen years old. The statistics on adults vary a lot, but they show that the majority of people—male or female—have masturbated at least once. Although more guys than girls masturbate, and although guys tend to do it more often, it's normal for everyone. We all have sexual urges and a desire to get to know our bodies sexually, and masturbation is a healthy way to do that.

And it's okay to masturbate as often as you like, even if it's more than once a day. It's normal for teenagers to become especially aware of their sexual feelings and want to masturbate often. It's healthy as long as it doesn't interfere with the rest of your life (it should not keep you from doing other important stuff like homework or hanging out with your friends) and as long as it's something you do in private or with a consenting partner.

JACKING (AND JILLING) OFF: A HOW-TO

There is no right or wrong way to pleasure yourself sexually, but there are some common methods. One of the most common methods guys use to masturbate is to stroke their hand up and down their penis. Some like to focus attention on the glans, which is the head of the penis (found on the diagram on page seven) because it's especially sensitive, while others might find it *too* sensitive for a lot of stimulation. Some guys like to play with their testicles; others may like to stick a finger up their anus (yes, really). Many guys also like to use a type of lubricant like lotion, baby oil, or K-Y Jelly when masturbating.

With girls things can be a little trickier. She may rub her clitoris, usually the most sensitive part of her anatomy. Or, if her clitoris is very sensitive and rubbing it is too intense, she might rub the area around it—her labia, her clitoral hood—which will indirectly stimulate her clitoris. She may also put a finger (or something else) insider her vagina while she masturbates. Or she may do some combination of all these things. She may also touch her breasts or other areas that feel good. Whichever method works is the best method.

While masturbation is normal and harmless, it *can* cause problems if experiments get out of hand. Guys sometimes have the urge to put their penis in something besides their hand—a cantaloupe, a pie, a vacuum cleaner. It's possible this could lead to infection or, in the case of the vacuum cleaner, dismemberment. And girls sometimes want to put something inside the vagina—a long, thin vegetable like a cucumber, perhaps. Again, this could put her at risk for infection if the object isn't cleaned carefully first. Make sure you use common sense. Don't let anything unclean touch your genitals, and if necessary, rinse yourself off afterward.

When you masturbate, you'll probably start to fantasize, which is a great way to get to know what turns you on. It's okay to think about anything that arouses you while you're masturbating, no matter how strange or outlandish it may be. Your fantasies are your own, and there's no reason to feel guilty about them. Acting on them is a different story—it is only appropriate to live out fantasies if you can do so safely and with the consent of your partner. But when it comes to your own private thoughts, the sky's the limit.

QUESTIONS

I masturbate, but I believe it's wrong. Please help me stop!

Lots of people believe it's wrong to masturbate. Some believe their religion forbids masturbation. Others may have been taught that it's wrong by their parents. And lots of people just feel guilty doing it, though they don't know why. But here's the thing: The only thing masturbation does is make you feel good, and it doesn't hurt anyone.

You may have gotten the message from your parents that masturbation is not okay. Sometimes if kids are caught touching their genitals when they're very little, parents want to tell them that it's not okay to do this in front of other people, but they end up sending the message that it's not okay at all, and kids grow up feeling ashamed about it. But the truth is, masturbation is common and harmless.

Some people try to stop masturbating, but it's usually a tough habit to break. I can't help you stop masturbating—I don't know of any twelve-step programs for this like there are for drug addiction. The only thing I can do is tell you that you have found a safe and healthy outlet for your sexual feelings. Rather than quit, try accepting that masturbating means you're a normal person with normal sexual urges.

Can masturbation affect my sex life? Will it make it less likely that I will enjoy sex with a partner?

If you masturbate, it's more likely you know what it takes to make you feel good. You can then share this information with your partner. Masturbation is not very likely to prevent you from enjoying sex with someone else—it may actually make it better, because you'll know more about your body.

Is it okay to use vibrators to masturbate?

Lots of people use vibrators (plastic or silicone toys that use electricity or batteries to vibrate) during masturbation, because they can provide sensations that your hand can't. Lots of vibrators are shaped like penises, but many others aren't—lots of women prefer to feel vibrations on their clitoris, rather than inside the vagina. Either way, a vibrator can be a new and different way to stimulate yourself. And if you've never had an orgasm, a vibrator may provide enough stimulation to help you have one.

If you use vibrators, be sure to wash them with soap and water after each use, and keep them in a clean place. You should never share a vibrator with a friend without boiling it in water for five minutes first. (If your vibrator is electrical, though, never let it be wet and plugged in at the same time!) And finally, if you enjoy inserting toys into your anus, make sure you only do this with toys specifically designed for this purpose. "Butt plugs" are sex toys that are much bigger at one end, so that they can't get lost inside the anus. In addition, anything that goes into a butt should be washed carefully before it goes into a vagina or anywhere else. (Another way to keep vibrators clean and safe is to put condoms on them.) As long as you keep your toys clean, it's safe to use vibrators to learn more about what sensations make you feel good.

Keep in mind that in most states, you have to be eighteen (or in some places even twenty-one) to enter a sex-toy store without an adult, and you have to be eighteen to view sex-toy sites online. There are also a few states in which it's illegal for anyone to sell sex toys.

Don't Let The Bed Bugs Bite: Sexually Transmitted Diseases

• •

AS WE DISCUSSED IN CHAPTER 4, HAVING SEX CARRIES WITH IT A LOT of responsibilities. One of the most important ones is protecting yourself and your partner from sexually transmitted diseases—diseases that can be passed from person to person through sexual contact.

If you're sexually active you should always have protected sex (see chapter 5 to learn more), and even if you do, get tested regularly—no form of protection is 100 percent effective. If you have a regular, exclusive partner, consider getting tested together and waiting until you both have clean test results before you put STD protection aside. And know that your health and that of your partner depend on honesty. If you don't agree to be exclusive, or aren't confident both of you will be, consider using STD protection just in case. You can be sure that *you* will always use condoms when you have sex, but if your partner has sex with other people, you'll have to trust that he or she will always be safe as well. Think about this: When you have sex with someone, you're at risk for any STD he or she has. If your partner has sex with someone else, you're at risk for any STD *that* person has as well (and any STD that person's *other partners* have, and so on).

This chapter cannot take the place of a visit to a doctor if you need one. It's impossible to diagnose and treat an STD yourself. Many STDs don't have symptoms. If you do have symptoms, you can't determine what they indicate without a test. And if you have an STD, you need proper treatment. If you think you may have an STD—either because you see symptoms that concern you or because you have had sex with someone who you think may be infected—visit a doctor or clinic right away. (See chapter 15 for help finding places that can test and treat you.)

HOW DO YOU KNOW IF YOU HAVE AN STD?

There are many warning signs that *might* indicate you have an STD. They include:

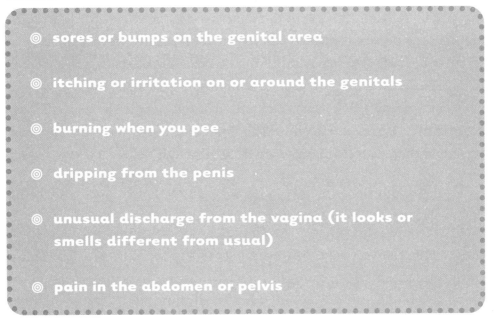

◎ sores or bumps on the genital area

◎ itching or irritation on or around the genitals

◎ burning when you pee

◎ dripping from the penis

◎ unusual discharge from the vagina (it looks or smells different from usual)

◎ pain in the abdomen or pelvis

If you experience any of these symptoms, you should see a doctor or visit a clinic as soon as possible. However, the most common symptom of any STD is no symptom at all. So most people who have an STD don't know they have one until they get tested.

HOW CAN YOU TELL IF YOUR PARTNER HAS AN STD?

If you notice anything suspicious around their genitals—sores, bumps, unusual discharge, an odor—that could be a sign of disease. But just as you can't always tell if *you* have an STD just by looking, you often can't tell if someone else does either.

It is possible to get an infection from sex with someone who has had no partners before you. For example, herpes is a virus that is characterized by cold sores, and it gets transmitted when a person comes in contact with someone else's sores. It can be transmitted through sex, but it can also be transmitted mouth to mouth by kissing when sores are on the mouth. So a person could have herpes even if they've never had sex—in fact some people grow up with it from the time they're babies. They could then pass the virus on to a partner's mouth or genitals.

Hepatitis and HIV can be transmitted when people share needles for IV drug use. A person who contracted one of these viruses through drug use could then pass them on to a partner through sex.

CAN YOU GET ANY STDS FROM KISSING?

Most STDs are transmitted through oral, anal, or vaginal sex—kissing is considered relatively safe. However, herpes and syphilis, which are most easily passed on when sores are present, can be transmitted mouth to mouth. Syphilis can be cured with medication, but herpes cannot. Someone with herpes should refrain from kissing while they are having an outbreak and right before they have an outbreak—they can learn to recognize the signs (such as a tingling sensation) that one is coming on.

HOW SAFE AM I IF I ALWAYS USE A CONDOM?

Condoms are great at protecting against certain STDs, like chlamydia, gonorrhea, and HIV, which live in semen and vaginal secretions. This is because condoms keep your fluids from coming in contact with your partner and vice versa. In those cases, if you use a condom properly every time, they can be extremely effective.

Condoms are less effective at protecting against STDs that can be transmitted through skin-to-skin contact, such as herpes, HPV, or syphilis.

- Someone with *herpes* has periodic, usually painful outbreaks of open sores in clusters on the skin around their genitals or mouth.

- Someone with *HPV* may have warts (hard, rough lumps) on their genitals.

- The symptoms of *syphilis* include a painless sore called a chancre.

It's more difficult to protect against these STDs because a condom will only cover the penis, leaving the surrounding area exposed. So, for example, if you're a guy having vaginal sex with a girl, even if you use a condom, the skin around your penis will come in contact with the skin on her vulva. The same would be true for anal sex.

I THINK I MIGHT HAVE AN STD. WHAT SHOULD I DO?

If you think you might have an STD, see a doctor or visit a clinic immediately. Even if the symptoms go away by themselves, get them checked anyway—this doesn't mean you aren't still infected. Until you get checked and treated, you should not have sex.

If you know who gave you the infection, tell that person if possible. They may not know that they are infected. If there's any chance you passed it along—if you had sex with someone after the time you think you were infected—do them the courtesy of telling them to get checked as well.

STD Testing

Some STDs, such as HIV, syphilis, and hepatitis, can be diagnosed through a blood test. Others, like gonorrhea and chlamydia, require a swab of the urethra or vagina. If you want to be tested for STDs, you can see your doctor, or go to an adolescent health clinic or your local Planned Parenthood. Or call your local Department of Health to find a place to test—there are lots of places that will do it for free.

Girls may also be tested as part of their annual GYN exam. Check with your gynecologist to see if you are being routinely tested.

Confidentiality policies for people under eighteen can vary depending on your location. For specific information on your area, you can contact the Department of Health in your area, or contact your state's American Civil Liberties Union (www.aclu.org).

For certain STDs—hepatitis, chlamydia, gonorrhea, syphilis, and HIV—a positive result needs to be reported to your state Department of Health for counting purposes. However, this information is kept confidential there, and it is not released to anyone else.

doing it right

Whatever you do, don't let confidentiality get in the way of you getting tested immediately. Find a way to get tested that is comfortable for you as soon as you can.

QUESTIONS

What's a urinary tract infection?

Any part of your urinary tract—the bladder, kidneys, or urethra—can get infected, usually due to bacteria. UTIs are more common in girls because they have shorter urethras than guys. You can get them during sex, when bacteria from the anus get pushed toward the urethra (though they don't always occur because of sex). Condoms can help prevent UTIs. Another way to prevent them is to pee right after having sex, to flush bacteria away before it travels into the urethra. A doctor can test for a urinary tract infection by looking at a sample of your urine, and it can be treated with antibiotics. You can also help treat it by drinking lots of water and cranberry juice (preferably unsweetened because sugar can make the infection worse), but don't attempt to treat a UTI alone.

What are yeast infections, and why do girls get them?

A yeast infection occurs when yeast that is normally found in the vagina starts to overgrow. They're very common—most women will get at least one in their lifetime.

Yeast infections are rarely transmitted through sex. They're usually caused by hormonal changes or by antibiotics. Girls may also be at risk if they're using an IUD or scented sanitary napkins or tampons, which most doctors don't recommend.

Some signs you're getting a "yeastie beastie" include itching or burning on the vulva, or a thick white discharge that looks a little like cottage cheese. It can be treated with creams or suppositories, which are inserted into the vagina, or by oral medicines.

Some people are just more susceptible to yeast infections than others. If you discover you're one of those people, listed below are a few ways to avoid them. It's rare that you can pass a yeast infection on to a guy, but to be safe it's best not to have sex till you're infection-free.

◎ **Wear cotton underwear, rather than satin (it breathes better).**

◎ **Avoid wearing tight pants.**

◎ **Eat plenty of yogurt—it contains *Lactobacillus acidophilus*, a bacteria that helps fight off yeast infections.**

◎ **Take acidophilus pills, which you can find in most health food stores (consult a doctor before doing this).**

◎ **Try cutting down on sugar and see if it helps.**

◎ **If your doctor prescribes antibiotics for an illness, be aware that a yeast infection might pop up and be prepared—for example, try eating some yogurt to ward off an infection before you even get one.**

What's HPV, and how do I prevent it?

There are about one hundred different types of human papilloma virus, and about thirty of them affect the genitals. Most strains of the virus don't cause symptoms, but a few cause genital warts—soft white bumps that may be itchy—and a few others can lead to cancer in the cervix, vulva, or penis.

HPV can be spread through oral, anal, and vaginal intercourse. Using a condom helps, but because the virus can be transmitted through skin-to-skin contact, condoms aren't as effective as they can be with viruses that are transmitted through fluids.

A person who has genital warts can be diagnosed with HPV on sight. Also, abnormal cervical cells detected during a Pap test at an annual gyn exam can sometimes indicate HPV infection. If you do get an abnormal Pap result, you'll need to return for a follow-up Pap, which will most often be normal. There is no way to test a guy for this disease, and since most guys don't have symptoms, guys rarely know if they have it.

There's no treatment for HPV—the virus usually goes away by itself within several months or a year. If you have a type of HPV infection that causes warts, they can be removed.

A vaccine against some types of HPV called Gardasil was recently approved for girls ages nine to twenty-six. It's expected to be recommended to girls before they become sexually active, because that's when it's most effective.

HIV AND AIDS

HIV stands for *human immunodeficiency virus*. To break that down:

> **HUMAN:** Only people get this particular virus, and only people can pass it on to others.
>
> **IMMUNODEFICIENCY:** Your immune system is made up of all the parts in your body that help you fight disease. Immunodeficiency means that the immune system is deficient—that it isn't working as well as it should be.
>
> **Virus:** A type of germ.

HIV is the virus that causes AIDS. AIDS stands for acquired immune deficiency syndrome.

> **ACQUIRED:** You have to get HIV from someone else.
>
> **IMMUNE DEFICIENCY:** The immune system is not working as well as it should be.
>
> **SYNDROME:** A group of symptoms and illnesses.

HIV is a virus that can be transmitted from person to person. A person with HIV may feel perfectly healthy—in fact, they may not even know they have the virus unless they get a test. However, in an average of ten years, most people with HIV develop illnesses: Their immune systems become very weak, and their bodies are no longer able to fight off illnesses that healthy people fight every day. At this point, they are diagnosed with AIDS.

HIV gets from one person to another through four fluids:

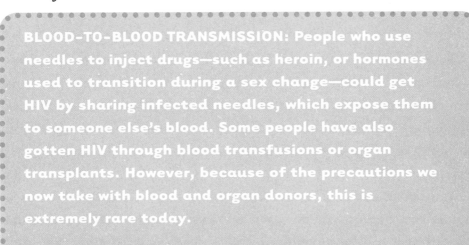

Blood

Semen (and pre-cum)

Vaginal secretions (the fluids from inside the vagina)

Breast milk

These are the only fluids that transmit HIV. Saliva, tears, sweat, pee, snot, and any other fluid you can think of do not transmit HIV.

There are a number of ways the fluids that contain HIV can get from one body to another:

BLOOD-TO-BLOOD TRANSMISSION: People who use needles to inject drugs—such as heroin, or hormones used to transition during a sex change—could get HIV by sharing infected needles, which expose them to someone else's blood. Some people have also gotten HIV through blood transfusions or organ transplants. However, because of the precautions we now take with blood and organ donors, this is extremely rare today.

MOTHER-TO-CHILD TRANSMISSION: A mother who has HIV may pass it along to her unborn child during pregnancy, child birth, or breast-feeding.

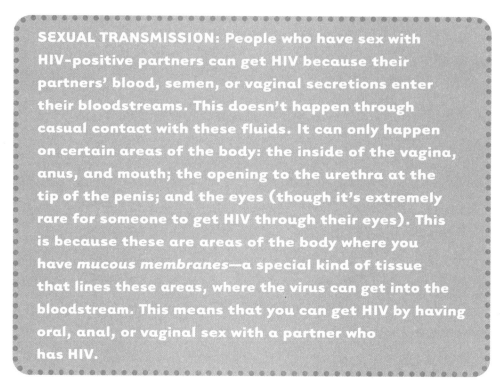

SEXUAL TRANSMISSION: People who have sex with HIV-positive partners can get HIV because their partners' blood, semen, or vaginal secretions enter their bloodstreams. This doesn't happen through casual contact with these fluids. It can only happen on certain areas of the body: the inside of the vagina, anus, and mouth; the opening to the urethra at the tip of the penis; and the eyes (though it's extremely rare for someone to get HIV through their eyes). This is because these are areas of the body where you have *mucous membranes*—a special kind of tissue that lines these areas, where the virus can get into the bloodstream. This means that you can get HIV by having oral, anal, or vaginal sex with a partner who has HIV.

Everyone—gay or straight, male or female—can get HIV from sex. You can prevent HIV by using a condom, a female condom, or a dental dam (all described in chapter 5) every time you have sex, or by sticking to other kinds of sexual activity that don't put you and your partner in contact with each other's fluids, such as kissing, touching, and massaging.

You *cannot* get HIV by putting a finger inside a partner's anus or vagina, or by getting their semen or vaginal secretions on your hand. You can't get it from hugging or kissing (even deep kissing). You can't get it from sharing food or utensils, or from a toilet seat or a mosquito bite. The only way you can get HIV from someone is by having sex with them or sharing a needle with them.

If You Think You've Been Exposed

If you are worried you were exposed to HIV in the last two to three days (you had unprotected sex or the condom broke) you have one emergency option. Go to a doctor or emergency room and ask them if you're eligible for postexposure prophylaxis, or PEP, which is a regimen of drugs that can prevent you from becoming HIV-positive right after an exposure. A doctor can call the PEP hotline at 1-888-448-4911, twenty-four hours, seven days a week (it's a good idea to have this number with you in case the doctor isn't aware of this hotline) to see if you qualify for these drugs.

If you were exposed to HIV more than two or three days ago, read the next section to learn about testing.

Testing for HIV

There are a number of different types of tests for HIV. Some involve taking a sample of the cells inside your mouth, while others require pricking your finger to take a small sample of blood. With a rapid test you can get your results within an hour; others require you to return to the center within a week or two to get your results. Call your testing center or look them up online to find out what kinds of tests they offer.

Once the results are ready, your tester will meet with you to discuss them. Here's what your results mean:

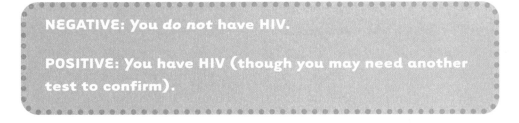

NEGATIVE: You *do not* have HIV.

POSITIVE: You have HIV (though you may need another test to confirm).

> **INCONCLUSIVE TEST:** This is very rare; it usually means you don't have HIV, but you must test again to be sure.
>
> **PRELIMINARY POSITIVE:** This result only occurs with a rapid test—it usually means you *do* have HIV, but you must take another test to confirm.

Make sure you understand your result and whether or not you need a follow-up test.

When to Test

The test for HIV looks for **antibodies** to HIV. Antibodies are the cells your body makes in response to an illness, to try to fight it off. It takes your body some time to make antibodies. So if someone was exposed to HIV today and took a test tomorrow, their result would probably not show the virus even if they had gotten it—their body would need more time to make antibodies.

It takes a person somewhere between one and three months to make enough antibodies to get a positive test result. This is called the window period for HIV testing.

If you are concerned that a particular sexual encounter exposed you to HIV, you can take a test as soon as one month afterward. But in order to be sure you don't have HIV, you should make sure you take another test three months after that encounter. If that result says you don't have it, then you did not get HIV from that encounter. If you are unsure about when to test, talk to someone at an HIV testing center, or call one of the HIV hotlines in chapter 15.

doing it right

Where to Test

You can test at an adolescent health center, a Planned Parenthood, or any clinic that tests for HIV. If possible, try to find out in advance if the place offers pre- and post-test counseling. This means that before the test, the tester will talk with you about why you have chosen to test for HIV and why you think you may be at risk. He or she will make sure you understand how to protect yourself from HIV if you don't have it already and discuss what you plan to do in the event that you do have HIV. After the test, you will discuss your result and your options for medical care and support in the event that you have HIV. You can also get an HIV test from a doctor during a regular check-up, but he or she cannot test you without your written permission. (You can find resources for HIV testing in chapter 15.)

Confidentiality for HIV Testing

HIV tests are confidential. This means that the person testing you cannot tell your results to anyone. (If you are under eighteen and want to know what your rights are in terms of keeping your HIV test private from your parents, check out your local ACLU for more information at www.aclu.org.) If you get a positive result—meaning you do have the virus—your name will be reported to the Department of Health for statistical purposes. However, that information cannot be revealed to anyone.

There are also places that can test for HIV anonymously—meaning that you do not have to give your name in order to get the test and your results will not be reported to the Department of Health. In this case, you would be given a number, so your results would not be attached to your name in any way.

Most places that test for HIV are confidential but not anonymous. If you want to have an anonymous test, call the Department of Health in your state for information.

12 What the Heck Does That Mean? Some Definitions

Definitions

SEX CAN BE A REALLY UNCOMFORTABLE SUBJECT, AND ONE WAY PEOPLE try to disguise that discomfort is by using slang. When words are especially charged, or sound too technical, or just make us feel weird, we use terms that are less charged in their place. These terms are constantly changing, but they're always easier to say than the technical terms we're trying to avoid. Let's face it—it's often easier to say "cooch" or "pussy" than "vagina," somehow more comfortable to get out "dick" or "cock" than "penis."

The trouble is, sometimes you don't know what these slang terms mean. But if it seems like everyone else does, you're reluctant to ask anyone. This chapter is a guide to some of the most common sex slang I've been asked about. Hopefully knowing what they mean will make talking about sex a little less uncomfortable.

Keep in mind that some slang terms can be offensive—just as there are derogatory slang terms for people of every race, there are also insulting slang terms for sex acts, body parts, and different sexual populations (gay and straight people, for example). If you don't know what a word means, don't repeat it without finding out more information. When in doubt, feel free to use the proper terms used in this book. If you can refer to your nose as your nose, there's no reason not to call a penis and a vagina by their real names, too.

ACTION: Any kind of sexual activity, as in "I got some action last night"; also known as "play."

BLOW JOB: A term for oral sex on a guy—meaning sucking or licking the penis. Oral sex may also be described as "going down on someone," or when performing it on a girl, "eating her out."

BLUE BALLS: Discomfort or pain a guy may feel when he's turned on for a long time without having an orgasm. While he may be uncomfortable, this won't cause damage to his penis, testicles, or brain. If you're with a guy who's complaining about blue balls, you have no obligation to have sex with him! There are plenty of ways to relieve this problem—he can masturbate or, if you're comfortable, you can help him out with your hand without putting yourself at risk for STDs or pregnancy (see "hand job").

CUMMING: Reaching climax during sexual activity, either for a male or female, also known as an orgasm or "getting off." "Cum" is also a term for semen, which comes out of a guy's penis when he ejaculates. You can read more about all this in chapter 13.

DOGGY STYLE: Having vaginal or anal sex with someone from behind, like dogs usually do.

DRY HUMPING: Simulating sex (pressing your pelvis against your partner's) with clothing still on.

FAMILY JEWELS: Another term for the testicles or "balls."

FRIENDS WITH BENEFITS: A friend you fool around with, as opposed to a boyfriend or girlfriend you're committed to.

FOREPLAY: Sexual activity—kissing and touching—that occurs before two people have intercourse, kind of like a warm-up before a workout.

FRENCH KISS: Kissing that involves mouths open and tongues touching.

GETTING HARD: What happens to a guy when he gets sexually aroused. More blood flows to the genitals, and the penis gets bigger and harder. This is technically called an erection, but you may hear people refer to getting a hard-on, boner, or woody.

GETTING WET: What happens when a girl gets sexually aroused. This happens for the same reason guys get hard—more blood flow to the genitals. The blood that flows to the vagina pushes fluid to the surface of the walls, making her wet inside. This provides natural lubrication during intercourse.

doing it right

HAND JOB: Stimulation of a guy's penis with your hand—similar to what he might do himself when he masturbates. This is a very safe way to satisfy a guy without putting yourself at risk for STDs, including HIV, and pregnancy.

HICKEY: The mark that occurs if you kiss/suck/nibble on one spot long enough to break some blood vessels. The reddish mark that is left behind is harmless, and it'll go away in a few days.

HOOKING UP: Depending on who you talk to, this could mean anything from making out to having sex.

HORNY: A feeling of craving sex, as in, "Reading about sex in this book is making me horny."

JACKING OFF: Masturbation—or as some like to call it, "whacking off," "jerking off," "spanking the monkey," "choking the chicken," or "rubbing one out." You might notice that most of these sound like they apply to guys. There aren't too many terms that specifically apply to girls, so as the counterpart to jacking off, I propose "jilling off."

MORNING WOOD: The erection guys often wake up with in the morning.

PRE-CUM: A few drops of clear fluid that may come out of a guy's penis before he ejaculates (also known as pre-ejaculate). Its purpose is to clean out the urethra and provide a little extra lubricant for sex. Some guys have pre-cum and some don't—either way, it's normal. Just like semen, pre-cum can contain enough sperm to get a girl pregnant and can transmit STDs. This is one reason why having a guy pull out before he ejaculates is not a good way to practice safer sex.

POPPING THE CHERRY: Breaking the fold of tissue inside the vagina, called the hymen. This layer is often torn the first time a girl has vaginal sex, though it can also tear as a result of anything being inserted into the vagina—like a tampon or fingers. When the hymen is broken during sex, that's sometimes referred to as "popping the cherry." It's normal for this to cause some pain or bleeding.

QUEEF: The sound that occurs when air trapped inside the vagina during sex is released. It may sound a lot like a fart, and it can be embarrassing, but it happens to everyone at some point.

SIXTY-NINE: A sexual position in which two people are giving each other oral sex at the same time—named because it looks just like a 69.

Ohh Is for Orgasm

13

WHAT HAPPENS WHEN YOU GET SEXUALLY AROUSED?

YOUR BODY RESPONDS TO SEXUAL STIMULATION—WHETHER YOU'RE getting it on with someone else or by yourself—in five stages.

Desire is simply the feeling of wanting sex. You may feel desire when you're with someone you're attracted to, or you may just have a general feeling of wanting to be sexual.

During **excitement** the body becomes more sensitive to touch. Heart rate and breathing get faster, and blood rushes to the genitals. In guys this means the penis gets hard. In girls the blood pushes fluid toward the walls of the vagina, making it swollen and wet. You may feel throbbing in your genitals and a tingly sensation all over. Nipples may become erect and sensitive, though this is more common in girls than in guys.

During **plateau** the body continues to be very sexually aroused. This is when some guys release pre-cum, a few drops of clear fluid from the penis. In girls the inside of the vagina expands, which can sometimes create a hollow feeling. Many girls, and some guys, will get what is called "sex flush"—what looks sort of like a rash on the skin of their chests, stomach, or butt.

Orgasm is the climax of sexual excitement—it's a very pleasurable sensation that originates in the genitals but can be felt all over the body. An orgasm is a series of muscle contractions that result from the tension that has been building up as you've become aroused. In guys the muscles in the penis contract, pushing out semen. In girls the muscles in the uterus, vagina, and fallopian tubes contract. In both guys and girls the muscles of the anus contract as well. While there are obviously lots of differences, males and females tend to describe their orgasms very similarly.

Orgasm is followed by a stage called **resolution**, in which the body returns to the unaroused state and the blood resumes flowing normally.

If you start to pay attention, you'll notice how your body responds when you're aroused. You can recognize these responses as a sign that you're turned on. Notice when you feel aroused and when you *don't*—your body is sending you signals about whether or not you're feeling sexual.

The Female Orgasm

Most of the time it's easy to tell when a guy has an orgasm—he usually ejaculates when he does. The evidence is not always so clear for a girl's orgasm. If a girl is not sure if she's had one, then my guess is that she probably hasn't, because it's usually unmistakable when it happens. She may feel her vagina contract, which kind of feels like a series of squeezes. Some say they feel a sensation of their vagina or their whole pelvis opening up.

If your partner is a girl and you're wondering how to tell if she's had an orgasm, the best thing to do is ask her! She will most likely appreciate this—it will show her that you're interested.

Some girls orgasm very easily, while others need to spend a while learning how. I know women who had their first orgasm as young girls with hardly any effort, and others who passed thirty without ever having one, despite hours of trying. So girls who have never had one should be patient. Chances are a girl is capable of having one if she spends some time figuring out how her body works. Some people find it easier to do this when they're alone and not feeling rushed or worried about being interrupted. She should get relaxed and comfortable, and focus her mind on feelings and sensations rather than thoughts. Fantasizing will help too.

A girl usually has an orgasm by stimulating the clitoris, rather than the vagina. The clitoris contains a lot of nerve endings in a very small space, making it very sensitive. Some girls don't like direct stimulation there—it can provide so much sensation that it actually hurts. If that's the case, she needs to figure out what *doesn't* hurt. Touching other parts of the vulva can indirectly stimulate the clitoris, which some girls prefer. Or she may want to touch her clitoris very gently. It will take some experimentation to see what works best.

She may also discover that her body responds differently to masturbation depending on the time of day, how relaxed she feels, or where she is in her menstrual cycle. And even after she figures out how to have an orgasm, she may not be able to have one any time she wants to. The body is pretty complicated. But she can learn a lot by experimenting. And although most sexually active people are interested in having orgasms, they are not the only pleasurable thing about sex by far. She should not let the lack of orgasms keep her from enjoying her body, whether it's by herself or with a partner.

For more thoughts on this subject, I recommend the book *Sex for One* by Betty Dodson.

The Male Orgasm

While girls usually ask me how to have an orgasm, guys usually want to know how to keep from having one too soon. Lots of guys ejaculate pretty quickly their first few times having sex, when things are very new and very exciting. Once a guy is a little more experienced, he should be able to last longer. One thing that may help guys do this, interestingly enough, is a condom, because it may reduce the sensation of sex a little bit.

After a guy has an orgasm, his penis usually gets softer and smaller again. It may be very sensitive to the touch, and it may be a while before he can get hard again. This "refractory period" is completely normal—it's just his body's way of recharging after the hard work of having an orgasm.

QUESTIONS

I can have orgasms, but only by masturbating, not during vaginal sex. Is that normal?

Yes, it's normal. In fact, most girls *don't* have orgasms through vaginal intercourse (without additional stimulation). This is because most girls have orgasms from clitoral stimulation, and vaginal sex doesn't usually provide enough sensation to the clitoris for her to orgasm.

If you want to have an orgasm during sex, there are plenty of solutions: One of you could stimulate your clitoris during sex, for example, or you might reach orgasm some other way. But the only way to figure that out is to talk to your partner. This might be a little embarrassing, but it's important. You are the expert on what makes you feel good, and there's no reason to expect anyone to be able to figure it out on their own—no matter how many partners they've had in the past. Everyone is unique.

How do I tell my partner what will make me have an orgasm without feeling mortified?

If you find it a little intimidating to open up and say, "Hey, I'd really like it if you'd lick my earlobes right now," here are a few things to keep in mind:

- If it's too hard to say it out loud, try *showing* your partner what you want instead—lick *her* earlobes. If your partner is of the opposite sex, this may be a little difficult when it comes to some body parts, but be creative.

- Try masturbating in front of your partner. Let him watch the expert at work.

- Play "hot and cold"—let her guess where you want to be touched, and tell her when she's getting close to the right spot.

- When your partner does something that feels really good, let him know!

- Above all, have a sense of humor—it's supposed to be fun.

If a guy doesn't have an orgasm for a long time, does the semen build up inside him? Could something bad happen?

No, not at all. You can kind of think of semen like blood—your body can make more when you need it, so you always have the right amount. If you release it, your body will make more. If you don't release it, you may be more likely to have a wet dream while you're asleep (see chapter 3 for more information on those) but that's about it. It's not going to get backed up and make you explode!

Is it possible for girls to ejaculate?

As you've read, when a girl is aroused the inside of her vagina becomes wet. This is *not* ejaculation; this is her vagina lubricating to make sex easier.

But girls *can* ejaculate. Most girls have a spot inside the vagina, on the front part (toward the belly button) about one third of the way up, called the G-spot. It may feel a little bumpy to the touch, like the surface of a walnut shell. When it's stimulated, it may feel a little like she has to pee, because it's so close to her urethra. Stimulating this spot can cause some girls to have an orgasm that feels different from an orgasm from clitoral stimulation. When that happens, she may ejaculate—liquid may spurt out of her urethra. However, the fluid is not urine—according to research, it seems to be similar to the fluid released by the male prostate.

This is a difficult spot for her to reach on her own because of the angle, and touching it may or may not cause an orgasm, and may or may not make her ejaculate.

Can a guy have an orgasm without stimulation to his penis?

Yes! You might remember that in chapter 2 we talked about the prostate, a part of the male anatomy that helps produce semen. You can't stimulate the prostate directly, but it may be stimulated indirectly during anal sex. If that happens, it's very pleasurable for a guy, pleasurable enough that he could have an orgasm even if there's no contact with his penis. Some guys may also feel sensation in their prostate when there's pressure applied to the spot between his testicles and his anus.

Rape and Sexual Abuse

14

THIS CHAPTER CONTAINS INFORMATION ABOUT THINGS THAT MAY sound scary. Fortunately, while the things I describe in this chapter do happen, they don't happen to most people, and they will be less likely to happen to you if you're aware of how to protect yourself.

WHAT IS RAPE?

Rape is any act of oral, anal, or vaginal sex without consent. In chapter 4 we talked about how someone knows they're ready to have sex. This is a decision only you can make, and you have the right to make it without influence from anyone else, including a potential partner. If you're in a situation where you feel you're being pressured to have sex, the word "no" should be enough to make the person stop. If they don't stop, it's rape.

Some myths about rape:

Myth: Someone who dresses in a sexy way is asking to be raped.

Fact: Someone who dresses in a sexy way is not asking to have sex against his or her will.

Myth: When a girl says no, she really means yes.

Fact: When people say no, they should be taken at their word.

Myth: If a person doesn't fight back, he or she wasn't raped.

Fact: People having sex against their will were raped, whether or not they have made the choice to fight back.

Myth: Rape is motivated by sexual urges.

Fact: Rape is an act of violence, not sex.

Myth: Sometimes people have sexual urges they can't control, and that's why rape happens.

Fact: A healthy person can control sexual urges.

Myth: If your date paid for dinner, if you are alone in a quiet place, or if you're making out, you're obliged to have sex with him or her.

Fact: No one is ever obliged to have sex with anyone.

Consent

Consent means you and your partner both freely agree to have sex. All sex should be consensual. Sex that involves threat or force—whether it's verbal or physical—is not consensual. A person who is drunk, on drugs, or unconscious cannot give consent for sex.

Someone who is under the legal age of consent in their state can't give consent either. A person who has sex with someone younger than the age of consent can be charged with **statutory rape**—that means it was rape according to the law even if both partners agreed to have sex. The age of consent in most state ranges between sixteen and eighteen. In some states it's different for boys and girls, and in some states it's different depending on whether the partners are of the same or opposite sex. Some states also take into account the difference between the ages of the partners involved. For information on your state, go to www.avert.org/aofconsent.htm.

Dressing in a sexy way does not mean you are consenting to sex. Kissing, flirting, or making out does not mean you are consenting to sex. You don't agree to have sex by going home with or getting a ride home from someone. You have a right to say no to sex no matter what and to have that decision respected.

Date Rape

Most rapes are date rapes, meaning they are committed by someone the victim knows. When you're dating someone new whom you don't know well, it's smart to avoid being alone with that person until you have been out a few times and feel comfortable. There are lots of ways you can enjoy dating without putting yourself at risk—try going out with a group of friends, double-dating with another couple, or meeting in public places. It's natural to want to be alone with your date, but take your time and don't put yourself at risk.

When you're on a date, be clear about what you want. Make sure you're not sending mixed messages; just say what you mean.

Going out on a date with someone—even if he or she pays—doesn't mean you are consenting to sex. You should only have sex if it's something you're sure you want to do. If you feel you're being pressured to have sex, say "no" firmly. This should always be enough to get the other person to stop. If you continue to feel pressured, leave as quickly as you can and go home or somewhere safe.

If you've experienced date rape, you probably consented to being alone with your attacker and maybe consented to some making out even though you didn't want to have sex. There may not be any evidence that you were forced. These things can make the situation unclear and could make it difficult to press charges if you choose to. But the bottom line is, sex against your will, whether it was because of physical force, a threat, or intimidation, is rape.

Date Rape Drugs

Rohypnol, GHB, and Ketamine are common date rape drugs, meaning they have been used to coerce unsuspecting people into having sex against their will. Rohypnol is the most common—you may have heard it referred to as "roofies." If these drugs are slipped into a drink, within roughly a half hour the victim may become dizzy, confused, seem drunk or high, and eventually pass out. When he or she regains consciousness, there will be no memory of what happened.

It's against the law for someone to give you a drug without you knowing it, whether they cause you any other kind of harm or not. If you suspect you have been given such a drug, get to an emergency room as soon as you can and get a urine test. These drugs leave the system quickly, so it's important to get a test as soon as you can.

This is a serious situation, but here's what you can do to avoid having it happen to you or your friends:

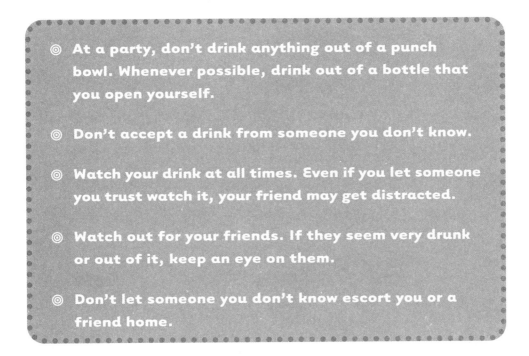

- At a party, don't drink anything out of a punch bowl. Whenever possible, drink out of a bottle that you open yourself.

- Don't accept a drink from someone you don't know.

- Watch your drink at all times. Even if you let someone you trust watch it, your friend may get distracted.

- Watch out for your friends. If they seem very drunk or out of it, keep an eye on them.

- Don't let someone you don't know escort you or a friend home.

Street Smarts

Although most rapes are committed by someone the victim knows, sexual assault by strangers does occur. Here are some ways to make sure it doesn't happen to you:

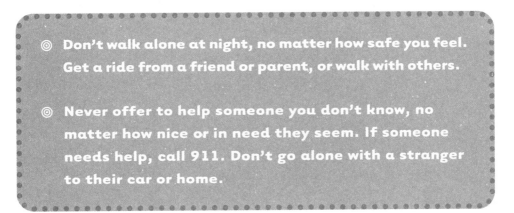

- Don't walk alone at night, no matter how safe you feel. Get a ride from a friend or parent, or walk with others.

- Never offer to help someone you don't know, no matter how nice or in need they seem. If someone needs help, call 911. Don't go alone with a stranger to their car or home.

- ◎ If you drive, don't walk through parking lots or garages by yourself at night or when there are few people around. You can always get a security guard to escort you if you don't feel safe.

- ◎ Be aware of your surroundings. Keep your eyes and ears open.

- ◎ Trust your gut instinct. If someone gives you a bad feeling—even if you're not sure why—listen to it.

- ◎ If someone does try to assault you, scream as loudly as you can. This will scare them off, get others to come help you, or both.

- ◎ If you feel it would be valuable to you, take a self-defense course. Many of these classes teach you more than just how to beat someone up; they teach you how to be aware and ward off an assault before it even happens.

If you have been a victim of rape, there are a few things you should do as quickly as you can:

- ◎ Get to a safe place and, if possible, call a friend for help.

- ◎ Get medical attention. Even if you don't feel you've been physically injured, you may have injuries you aren't aware of. A hospital can check you out, treat you if necessary, and perform a rape kit, which will help preserve evidence. If you have any reason to believe you were drugged, ask the hospital to collect a urine sample to be tested. You should also discuss the possibility of STD transmission, and if you are female, you should also be offered the option of emergency contraception (see chapter 6 for more information).

◎ Try to preserve evidence of the attack—don't eat, drink, wash your hands, bathe, or brush your teeth until after you've had medical attention.

◎ As soon as you can, write down as many details as you remember about the incident.

◎ Report the rape to the police. I realize this may be difficult, and it's up to you whether or not to do so, but it can help make sure your attacker doesn't harm others.

Once you've taken care of the most immediate concerns, find a professional you can talk to. Call the Rape, Abuse, and Incest National Network (RAINN) at 1-800-656-HOPE. Or call a local organization or professional counselor. Rape is something that takes time to deal with, and you can't deal with it alone.

Many rape victims blame themselves for their attack—but always remember that no matter what happened, you did not ask to be raped.

Being Safe Online

You don't remember a time when the Internet didn't exist, but it's actually a relatively new thing. It didn't exist when the adults you know were kids, which is why some of them are clumsier at using it than you are. Your parents didn't send their friends e-mail or chat with them on IM, and they didn't have a profile on MySpace.com. So they may also not be aware, as you should be, that what you do online potentially can be dangerous.

If you have an online profile or blog, be careful about what you post. It's easy to feel like the Internet is just a space to communicate with friends, but anything you post publicly can be seen and stored by anyone, whether you know them or not. Refrain from posting sexually explicit images or text. Make sure what you post doesn't include anything that could enable a stranger to track you down—like your full name, the name of your school, or where you tend to hang out. If you have a blog, consider limiting access and only letting people you know see it. If your blog or profile is public and you get comments that are mean, suggestive, or just make you feel uncomfortable, don't respond to them.

You should never get together in person with someone you met online, nor should you give such a person any personal information—your name, address, phone number, where you go to school. Nor should you ever send photos of yourself to people you don't know. If someone you meet online sends you anything that makes you feel uncomfortable, tell your parents. The Internet is a great place for people to prey on kids and teens because it gives people lots of opportunities to lie and deceive you. There is no way to know that what a person tells you about themselves—their age, their interests, etc.—is true.

I strongly discourage you from doing this, but if even after reading this, you absolutely must meet an online buddy face to face, meet in a public place like a café or mall, and do not go anywhere alone with the person or accept a ride anywhere. Tell a friend where you're going and let him or her know you'll call when the meeting is over, so someone will know when you're safe at home. Better yet, bring a friend with you. And above all, trust your instincts. If this person makes you uncomfortable or tries to persuade you to do anything you don't want to do, leave immediately and go somewhere safe.

Sexual Abuse

Sexual abuse can include any kind of unwanted sexual contact—whether it's rape (forced intercourse) or other kinds of sexual touching—and is usually committed by someone the person knows, often spends time with, and has begun to trust, like a parent, another relative, family friend, or teacher. If the abuser is related to the victim, it's called incest.

If you are in a situation where you are experiencing sexual abuse, it's important that you talk to someone. You need to find a way to make it stop and get emotional support for yourself. Even if this is something that happened a long time ago, it's never too late to talk about it. Consider talking to a counselor at your school or church, the parent of a friend, or another adult you trust. However, keep in mind that some adults are mandatory reporters. That means that if someone reports sexual abuse to them, they are required by law to report it to the police or child protective services. Teachers, doctors, and social workers are some examples of mandatory reporters—if you're not sure if someone is a mandatory reporter, you can ask them. Whether or not to report the abuse to the authorities is your choice.

HOW TO HELP A FRIEND

If you have a friend who tells you that they've been raped or sexually abused, you can help by being a good listener:

◎ Make sure he knows you believe him—it's very common for victims of sexual abuse to worry they won't be believed.

◎ Let her know you care and want to help, and that you will not tell anyone what she is sharing with you.

◎ Don't ask too many questions or press for details.

◎ Make sure he knows you don't feel this is his fault.

◎ Let your friend make her own decisions about how to handle the situation. People who experience sexual abuse often feel powerless; letting them choose what to do can help them regain a sense of control. Don't offer solutions; instead, ask her what she wants to do. She may not be ready to talk to anyone else besides you.

◎ That said, gently suggest that your friend talk with a rape hotline or counselor who can offer him more professional support. You can assist him in taking this step by offering him some phone numbers. He can call RAINN at 1-800-656-HOPE. You can also try to find out about resources in your area.

Know that you are doing a lot just by listening to your friend and believing what she tells you. And make sure that you have support too—dealing with a friend in trauma can be stressful for you as well.

doing it right

QUESTIONS

Is it true that people often lie about being raped?

No. Only a very small percentage of rape reports turn out to be false. And most of the rapes that occur are never reported. If someone tells you that he or she has been rapes, believe that person.

Can a guy be raped?

Yes. Guys can be raped by males or females.

Guys are much less likely than girls to report a rape—they may believe that rape is something that only happens to women, or they may be concerned that reporting a rape by a man will give others the impression that they themselves are gay (this can be uncomfortable for a straight guy, or for a gay guy who is not yet ready to come out). The truth is that anyone—male or female, gay or straight—can be raped.

As the result of rape, guys face the same feelings as girls—they may feel ashamed, powerless, scared, or angry. In addition, they may have a harder time finding support and a harder time being believed if they tell someone.

A common myth about male rape is that men who rape men are gay. The truth is that the vast majority of men who rape men are heterosexual. Again, rape is an act of violence, not sex.

I was raped a few years ago. Now I feel scared to get sexual with anyone. Will I ever be able to have a normal relationship?

Being the victim of sexual abuse is traumatic, and recovery is an ongoing process. You deserve ample time to work through this. As with any major trauma it takes time, support, and often counseling to work through the issues that arise.

It's very important that you talk with someone about how you're feeling—this is too much for you to deal with alone. I suggest you speak to a parent or another family member, a teacher, or any adult you feel comfortable confiding in, and ask for support in finding a rape counselor. In time, a professional or a psychiatrist who is trained in working with victims of sexual assault will help you deal with your issues surrounding the rape. There are also support groups that deal specifically with sexual abuse and rape. If you would like more information or would like help finding a therapist in your area, you can contact the Rape, Abuse, and Incest National Network (www.rainn.org) at 1-800-656-HOPE, twenty-four hours a day, seven days a week.

Rape is traumatic, but it is something people recover from. Whomever you choose to talk to, discuss your fears about sex. If you have a boyfriend or girlfriend, or if you get involved with someone, it might help for you to be honest with that person about what you're going through and ask for patience. Someone who cares about you can be a source of comfort rather than fear as you work through this. It's understandable that the thought of having sex is scary after what you have been through, but if you spend some time working through these issues you will be able to have a healthy, intimate relationship.

Where Can I Go for More Information? A Resource Guide

15

HERE'S A LIST OF BOOKS AND WEBSITES WHERE YOU CAN LEARN more about the topics discussed in this book.

SEXUALITY FOR TEENS

Websites

Doing It Right

www.doingitright.com

The Sex Lady offers more information and answers your questions.

TeensHealth

www.kidshealth.org/teen

Answers, advice, and straight talk for kids about sex and other aspects of health.

Advocates for Youth

www.advocatesforyouth.org

Strives to help young people make informed and responsible decisions about reproductive and sexual health.

TeenWire

www.teenwire.com

Planned Parenthood's website especially for teens.

Books

It's Perfectly Normal, by Robie H. Harris. Candlewick Press.
An illustrated book about puberty and reproductive health for kids.

Changing Bodies, Changing Lives, by Ruth Bell et. al. Three Rivers Press, 1998.
An encyclopedia of teen sexuality.

Sex, Puberty, and All That Stuff, by Jacqui Bailey. Franlin Watts Ltd., 2005.
The basics about sex, birth control, and STDs.

Deal With It, by Esther Drill, Heather McDonald, and Rebecca Odes. Pocket Books, 1999.
A book for girls by the women at gurl.com.

What's Going on Down There?, by Karen Gravelle with Nick Castro and Chava Castro. Walker Publishing, 1998.
A book for guys written by a woman and two teenage boys.

Sex for One, by Betty Dodson. Three Rivers Press, 1996.
A manual of masturbation.

Fiction

Forever . . ., by Judy Blume. Simon Pulse, 1975.

Doing It, by Melvin Burgess. Henry Holt and Co., 2006.

Love & Sex: Ten Stories of Truth for Teens, by Michael Cart. Simon Pulse, 2003.

Whores on the Hill, by Colleen Curran. Vintage, 2005.

PUBERTY

Websites

American Academy of Pediatrics
www.aap.org/family/puberty.htm

The American Social Health Association
www.iwannaknow.org/puberty

GAY, LESBIAN, BISEXUAL, AND QUESTIONING

Websites
Human Rights Campaign
www.hrc.org

Queer America
www.queeramerica.com

Parents and Friends of Lesbians and Gays
www.pflag.org

The Gay, Lesbian and Straight Education Network
www.glsen.org

National Youth Advocacy Commission
www.nyacyouth.org/nyac/youth_connections.html

Out Proud
www.outproud.org

Books
Nonfiction

What if Someone I Know is Gay? by Eric Marcus. Simon Pulse, 2007.
A question-and-answer book about gay and lesbian people.

Hear Me Out: True Stories of Teens Educating and Confronting Homophobia, by Planned Parenthood Toronto. Second Story Press, 2004.
Twenty-two stories from young people about their experiences.

GLBTQ: The Survival Guide for Queer and Questioning Teens, by Kelly Huegel. Free Spirit, 2004.
A guide for gay, lesbian, bisexual, transgender, and questioning teens, as well as for their straight peers and parents.

The Family Heart: A Memoir of When Our Son Came Out, by Robb Forman Dew. Ballantine Books; reprint edition, 1995.
The novelist explains her experience when her son Stephen came out.

Fiction

Rainbow Boys, by Alex Sanchez. Simon & Schuster, 2001.

Boy Meets Boy, by David Levithan. Knopf Books for Young Readers, 2005.

The Bermudez Triangle, by Maureen Johnson. Razorbill, 2005.

A Really Nice Prom Mess, by Brian Sloan. Simon & Schuster, 2006.

Letters in the Attic, by Bonnie Shimko. Academy Chicago, 2002.

A Tale of Two Summers, by Brian Sloan. Simon & Schuster, 2006.

TRANSGENDER, TRANS-SEXUAL, AND INTERSEX

Websites

Transgender support site
www.heartcorps.com/journeys

National Youth Advocacy Commission
www.nyacyouth.org/nyac/youth_connections.html

The Parents and Friends of Lesbians and Gays Transgender Network
www.pflag.org/PFLAG_s_Transgender_Network.tnet.0.html

Queer Bodies (for intersex youth)
www.queerbodies.org

Intersex Society of North America
www.isna.org

Books

Fiction

Luna, by Julie Ann Peters. Little, Brown Young Readers, 2004.

Parrotfish, by Ellen Wittlinger. Simon & Schuster Books for Young Readers, 2007.

BIRTH CONTROL AND PREGNANCY

Websites

To make an appointment at your local Planned Parenthood:
www.plannedparenthood.org
1-800-230-PLAN

To find out more about your rights when it comes to birth control:
www.covermypills.org

To get emergency contraception:
1-888-NOT-2-LATE

A state-by-state guide to laws on how to safely leave a baby:
www.guttmacher.org/statecenter/spibs/spib_IA.pdf

To find out parental notification laws for abortion in your state:
www.positive.org/Resources/consent.html

The American Civil Liberties Union, for information on privacy and your rights:
www.aclu.org

SEXUALLY TRANSMITTED DISEASES

Websites

For information on STDs and testing:

www.iwannaknow.org

www.advocatesforyouth.org/youth/health/stis/index.htm

www.plannedparenthood.org/sexual-health/stis-stds-101.htm

For testing sites in your area:

www.HIVgettested.org

www.knowHIVAIDS.org

For counseling and information on HIV/AIDS:

The Gay Men's Health Crisis (open to everyone)

www.gmhc.org

1-800-AIDS-NYC

RAPE AND SEXUAL ABUSE

Websites

Rape, Abuse, and Incest National Network

www.rainn.org

1-800-656-HOPE (4673)

911Rape

www.911rape.org

Child Help USA
www.childhelpusa.org

Male Survivor
www.MaleSurvivor.org

For laws on age of consent in each state:
www.avert.org/aofconsent.htm

Books

Fiction

Speak, by Laurie Halse Anderson. Puffin, 2001.

Inexcusable, by Chris Lynch. Atheneum, 2005.

Lucky: A Memoir, by Alice Sebold. Back Bay Books, 2002.

Index

doing it right

EVERYONE WONDERS, *WHAT WILL I DO WHEN I GROW UP?*

BUT HAVE YOU CONSIDERED:

Will I wear Prada or Old Navy to work?

*Would I rather play with kids on the playground,
or with bigwigs in the boardroom?*

Will I power lunch at the Ivy, or bag lunch at my desk?

What I can start doing right now to prepare?

Find the answers you really need,
from 50 inspiring women
who have the jobs of *your* dreams.

In Their Shoes
by Deborah Reber

Nonboring, Nonpreachy: Nonfiction

From Simon Pulse
Published by Simon & Schuster